Know Yourself Know Others—Joanne

I first met Joanne Antoun , during a period of my life when I knew changes were necessary but had no idea how to bring about those changes.

I was battling with mental illness (Bipolar Disorder) and the severe mood swings over a long period of time had left me confused, at times frightened and at other times totally despairing.

As well as that, the incredible highs that are on the other side of depression were also severe and my life as a result was spinning out of control.

Joanne has an amazing ability to connect with people, to clear a path and offer direction which can bring about a true transformation in the life of those that are blessed to meet her.

Joanne has a gift.

After our first meeting I knew that this was an opportunity for me to change some patterns which were holding me back and causing an increasing amount of dysfunction in my life.

A couple of healing sessions with Joanne , where she practiced Reiki, Emotional Freedom Technique and Neuro-Linguistic programming left me feeling different.

Within a couple of days of each session I felt invigorated, energized and more focused than I had been in long time.

I was on the road to changing myself and my life for the better.

My life today has balance.

Joanne Antoun has been a big part of that change.

It is so important for all of us to get to know ourselves and what makes us tick.

Joanne's new book "Know Yourself,Know Others " is a great place to start.

Enjoy!

Craig Hamilton
Author "Broken Open" and "A Better Life"
Motivational Speaker
Mental Health Advocate

Know Yourself, Know Others

The Thirty-Second Personality Type and Life Guide System

Joanne Antoun

BALBOA
PRESS

A DIVISION OF HAY HOUSE

Balboa Press books may be ordered through booksellers or by contacting:

Balboa Press
A Division of Hay House
1663 Liberty Drive
Bloomington, IN 47403
www.balboapress.com.au
1-(877) 407-4847

ISBN: 978-1-4525-1179-5 (sc)
ISBN: 978-1-4525-1180-1 (e)

Printed in the United States of America

Balboa Press rev. date:10/10/2013

Table of Contents

To you—and all those like you who care enough to work on their own personal development and consciousness, making our world a better place

Acknowledgements

It is with heartfelt love and gratitude that I wish to acknowledge my family, friends, students, clients, and all those who have been a part of my life's journey whether for a reason, a season, or a lifetime. You continually inspire me, and it is the moments with you that have blessed me with the knowledge and experience I now have.

To the wonderful team that have contributed to making this book possible from software design for the app right through to marketing. I thank you.

A special thank you to Elise Fee; your time, dedication, and tireless effort is what has made all of this possible. I am forever grateful.

To my beautiful daughter Ashleigh, my teacher and inspiration. You have blessed me with the role of mother, the greatest miracle that exists … that of life. Thank you for choosing me, and thank you for being the beautiful, inspiring angel that you are. I love you.

And finally, I thank you. I thank you for wanting to learn and grow for wanting to become a better person, and for making more empowered choices that will serve you, your personal evolution, and our planet.

Introduction

What lies before us and what lies behind us are small matters compared to what lies within us. When we bring what is within out into the world, miracles happen.
—Henry David Thoreau

My life's purpose and passion is to help people heal the past, live in the present, and create the future they desire. Empowering, motivating, and guiding people to "be the best they can be" is not only what I do—it is who I am.

As a teacher, public speaker, and therapist, I work with large numbers of people—and I couldn't help but begin to see common threads and patterns in people's personalities, behavioural tendencies, emotional issues, and reactions to life experiences.

While numerology isn't my focus and plays a very small part in my client sessions, over time, these common threads of how people perceive and approach life became glaringly evident.

People are my passion. I work with various modalities to help get you to where you need to be; however, true success and transformation occurs only when you are ready. And clearly you are ready today—ready to truly know yourself and ready to know others!

What Lies Within Us

You're about to take a magical journey that will help you uncover and discover many things about yourself.

- why you do the things you do
- how you perceive the world
- why people respond to you the way they do
- most importantly, how can you understand yourself and others better

What's exciting about the Life Guide System is that no matter how you live life (content with yourself as you are or always striving to grow and change), this system will apply to you and will help you really understand and know yourself on a deeper level.

> The descriptions for each type are written to encompass the gamut of possible evolution and growth stages for all people who fall under that particular type.

So whether you choose to live a highly evolved life or to go with the flow of where you are now, the type descriptions will help you comprehend your nuances and tendencies.

Let this be your map that helps you along your life's journey. The Life Guide System will tell you who you are and what drives you, yet your scope and potential for growth mentally, emotionally, and spiritually are limitless. You are capable of achieving the highest expression of your personality type and more!

As you read these descriptions, please keep in mind that there are levels of development within each personality type. You may, for instance, recognize aspects of yourself that were true in the past, some that are true now, and some that sound like they could be you in the future. We are constantly guided to become more conscious and aware, and the description of your type offers you the key to awareness and a map for where your road may be headed.

> What is described is the hidden force behind your personality; it is up to you to determine how you want to tap into your potential and utilize it.

The Life Guide System

The Life Guide System is a numerology-based system that allows you to quickly and easily determine other people's types as well as your own. Imagine how helpful it will be to know your boss's type, your significant other's type, or your mother's type!

There are some wonderful personality type systems available, including the Myers-Briggs Type Indicator (MBTI) and the Enneagram. Both can be complex and require you to complete a long questionnaire in order to discover your type. And having to complete a lengthy questionnaire makes it almost impossible to accurately discover someone else's type because you can't possibly answer correctly for someone else.

That's what makes this system so different! This tried and proven system, which has its roots in an ancient typology, enables you to determine your type—and anyone else's type—in a matter of seconds.

Using the System

We all have an innate desire for meaning, direction, and purpose in life, yet we get caught up in our own maps of reality and can't easily see how others view the world.

The Life Guide System gives you the keys to understanding yourself and others. It provides you with amazing insights into how you perceive and relate. These insights come not through your external behaviour (the face you show the world) but rather through the honest observation of your internal experiences—your motivations, beliefs, patterns of thinking, and feelings.

> Imagine having a better understanding of yourself—the what, who, how, and why questions can all be answered!

You will also learn the secrets of how you operate and why you do the things you do. More importantly, when you know what your strengths and weaknesses are, you can hone your strengths and evolve and improve upon your weaknesses.

In order for us to live up to our highest potential, we need to do more than just focus on our strengths. We must also acknowledge our weaknesses so we can grow from—and through—them.

When we gain a better understanding of our personality characteristics, this knowledge highlights and challenges the perception we have of ourselves and uncovers the games we tend to play. This gives us the opportunity to grow and make more empowered choices, choices that serve us, our personal evolution, and our world.

> Having a better understanding of yourself and others gives you the power to change everything in your personal and professional life.

It provides an opportunity to put aside your ego and gives you a better understanding of how others view the world, which ultimately creates better communication.

Enhance Communication and Clarity

Almost every aspect of our lives, at work and at home, is affected in one way or another by the ability to communicate. The outcome of every new initiative, every meeting, every interview, every sale, and every relationship, whether personal or professional—in fact, every single conversation—is dependent upon the quality of our communication.

Effective, high-quality communication strengthens relationships, improves team effectiveness, customer service, leadership skills, and problem-solving abilities, and has the power to reduce stress and conflict.

The ability to listen is just as important as communicating well. By understanding the person you are communicating with and his or her model of the world, you can become a better listener and learn how to adjust your words and tone so that the person can understand you clearly. Misunderstandings can be reduced and conversations can occur with clarity and acceptance of each person's worldview.

By increasing your awareness of unconscious patterns and motivations that may undermine you, you can choose to communicate more effectively with others, understand yourself better, and begin to know what drives other people to do the things they do.

These are just a few of the benefits gained by exploring how people perceive and interpret the world.

How the Life Guide System Works

Nothing happens by chance! The name you were given, the name you use now, and your date of birth all have significant meaning and vibrate at a particular frequency—and that creates the energy that makes you who you are.

Just as positive thoughts raise your vibration and allow you to attract a higher quality of life, so too is everything in our universe based on an energy or frequency.

With the Life Guide System, we use numerical values for your first name and add them to the numbers of the date you were born. In this way, a type number is determined that is aligned with your specific energy. (There is a very easy chart to figure this out and an iPhone and Android App titled Life Guide.)

Adding the numbers this way creates a particular type number that will help you understand how you think, how you rationalize things, why you do what you do, your mannerisms, idiosyncratic behaviours, etc.

While there are many tools of insight available, from both psychological and mystical traditions, the Life Guide System is a precise method.

> The system's strength lies in its relative simplicity and demonstrated effectiveness.

The origins of the Life Guide System date back to the Pythagorean School of ancient Greece. Pythagoras taught that numbers were the essence of all things. He spoke of cycles, patterns, and waves of energy, and he could see order where there seemed to be none. He noticed numerical patterns that perceptibly unlocked the secrets of our human psyche.

The Life Guide System was created while I was examining various numerology-based calculation methods in my efforts to simplify and bring together other widely available typology systems.

> This book simplifies what would normally require the calculations of many different combinations using your name and date of birth.

Doing so enables you to understand yourself in a comprehensive manner with a simple, single calculation method that takes mere seconds.

With the Life Guide System, you will delve deeper into who you are, what makes you tick, what your emotional drivers are, how you operate, how you think and perceive, and how you interpret life.

The Life Guide System

You will use the Life Guide System's calculation method to quickly determine your type. Each type has its own section in the book, providing you with:

- an in-depth exploration of who you are
- how and why you perceive your world the way you do
- your greatest fears and joys
- your gifts and talents
- your areas of weakness
- how you interact with others in your personal life, love life, and work life
- what others need to know to get along with you better
- questions you can ask yourself for growth and learning
- tips and affirmations for empowering yourself
- the phases of growth and evolution for your specific type

Once you've learned about yourself, take some time to calculate the types for your closest friends, colleagues, family members, co-workers, boss, past loves, etc. You will be amazed at how much insight you'll gain by reading about each of the types!

Let's get started!

Congratulations for taking this important step towards greater self-understanding and awareness.

> Clearly you are ready to learn profound insights about yourself and
> those with whom you interact.

The Life Guide System is the ideal tool to help you achieve a better understanding of yourself and others.

Enjoy the journey.

Discovering Your Personality Type

Calculating your Life Guide System Type

1	2	3	4	5	6	7	8	9
A	B	C	D	E	F	G	H	I
J	K	L	M	N	O	P	Q	R
S	T	U	V	W	X	Y	Z	

Nothing happens by chance! The name you were given, the name you use now, and your date of birth all have significant meaning and vibrate at a particular frequency—and that creates the energy that makes you who you are.

If the name given at birth and the name you use now is different it may be necessary to calculate the personality type for both to determine which frequency you carry.

Using your first name and the above chart, add the numerical value of each letter in your first name to the date of your birthday. Then keep adding until you reach a single digit.

For example: If your name is David and you were born on March 12, ignore the month and use the date to calculate.

(D = 4) + (A=1) + (V=4) + (I=9) + (D=4) + 1 + 2 = 25

Now take the final number (25 in this example) and add those digits together: 2 + 5 = 7. Thus, David is a personality Type 7.

Your journey begins now; simply turn to the appropriate chapter and get to know yourself and others.

Type One: The Instigator

I wish people would accept responsibility so that I don't have to do all the work.

You're best to avoid power struggles with me because I'm always right.

People really should make sure they've got everything covered.

No one ever does it as well as I do.

I hope they find this appropriate.

I would never sacrifice my morals.

At my best I'm loyal, dedicated, ethical, reliable, and helpful.

I should have checked the figures one more time.

I'm impatient and don't take criticism lightly.

At my worst in a relationship, I'm critical, argumentative, and uncompromising.

You want me to come to work on Sunday? That's fine.

1

Type One—The Instigator

As a Type One (the Instigator), you know what's right and how you want things to be. You are very conscientious, live up to your own set of high principles, and have a strong sense of ethics and morals. As a hopeful One, you feel a calling or sense of purpose and strive to use your influence to make things happen. You may find yourself teaching, advocating, or working to make the world a better place.

You enjoy overcoming challenges, especially moral ones, and want to see everyone's inner light shine brightly. Sometimes you'll feel inspired to make personal sacrifices to achieve your dreams. Some Ones will even leave a cushy life to do something they truly believe in. There are probably quite a few noble Ones in the Peace Corps!

You aim for perfection and get upset when you fall short of that lofty goal. As an organized, orderly worker, you have the ability to motivate yourself and work at something until it is successful, even if that means completely starting over on a project in order to get it right!

You don't take criticism lightly, and while you won't let others know how you're feeling, you get very angry when things don't work out the way you thought they should. Sometimes you don't even admit your anger to yourself. Nevertheless, you know that you feel worried and unhappy, even if you're not sure why.

> You have a tendency to be critical and perfectionistic.

As the impatient One, you can build up resentment and hold grudges—and you may even feel morally heroic in your efforts. When cornered, you may feel the need to justify yourself so that you are beyond criticism. Your worst fear is that you'll become corrupt.

3

At your best, you are an idealist and strive for the truth in all things. You work to make the world a better place and want to feel useful in some way. You enjoy taking practical steps towards your goals.

Others may perceive you as very private, self-controlled, or uptight, which is not at all how you feel inside.

> You feel so intensely that you worry you'll explode at someone!

When you become conscious of your feelings and learn to accept and process them in healthy ways, you are in an excellent position to teach others—through your words, and more importantly, through your example. When you learn to relax and laugh at yourself, life will flow much more easily for you.

In a Positive, Healthy State

Your truth-seeking nature drives you to do what's right and to make the world better for you having been in it. You think for yourself; when you follow your internal compass, you find the balance that you're seeking. When you fail to listen to your wise inner knowing, you will feel an increased need to be right, which can be problematic for you.

You enjoy making and following rules, having standards to adhere to, fulfilling your duties and responsibilities, putting work before pleasure, and earning deserved rewards. Be careful not to place too much attention on what's wrong, focus on others' mistakes, or dole out excessive punishments.

You excel at being an original, independent thinker, and you pride yourself on not being easily influenced by outside opinions or agendas. Employers value your beeline approach to solving problems and your dogged determination to stay focused on the project at hand. When pursuing your goals, be sure to look up occasionally and evaluate alternative approaches so you don't miss a turn and end up with a project that's going nowhere.

You love accuracy, details, thoroughness, and objectivity. At work, you want to be seen as respectable, responsible, hardworking, and sincere. You are a great person to have on a team because of your tireless attention to details that most others would rather not attend to.

> You are always working to improve yourself!

Something wonderful about you is that you try to act from your heart because you see that as the one truly perfect part of you.

In a Detrimental, Unhealthy State

When you are out of balance, your distaste for criticism becomes magnified, your sensitivity is heightened, and your unacknowledged anger bubbles up. You may find that you can't stop yourself from projecting those feelings onto others. You may catch yourself correcting others, secretly judging their actions, and launching an offense on the world in the hopes that it will keep you safe from what you anticipate to be people's eventual condemnation of you. Unfortunately, when you get to this place, your basic fears grow until you feel unsafe in life, which perpetuates this out-of-balance cycle.

When you fall out of balance, you might find yourself thinking in terms of black and white and using guilt-inducing language (should, must, ought to, have to, good, bad, perfect, not right, rules, policies, the right way, etc.). Some anxious Ones experience tightness in the body, especially in the neck, and may experience constriction and tension in the throat.

Compulsive Ones can succumb to eating disorders involving excessive dieting, vitamins, and cleanses. If you find yourself controlling your food intake to the extreme (bulimia or anorexia) or escaping through alcohol, it is proof that you are out of balance.

You have a strong internal voice that criticizes, judges, and corrects you. Most likely, you first heard this voice coming from a parent or other adult authority figure during childhood.

> You want to help others be perfect, which can get you into trouble
> and ruin relationships.

If you wish to get back to a positive healthy state, refrain from looking at others' mistakes and shortcomings; instead, reflect on your own truth. Go within for your safety and security—and remember to pursue the path that feels right and truthful to you. Simply start over. This is not hard for you to do because you do not give up easily!

There are times when you wish you could be more carefree and have fun. Be careful not to criticize yourself about this, too! Lightening up on your negative self-talk is the first step towards feeling freer.

Tips for Getting Along with Ones

You might want to share some important points with close friends and family or those with whom you work closely. These ideas may help others understand you better and teach them how best to interact with the principled One.

It's important to you that everyone carries his or her fair share of the workload and responsibility; otherwise, it feels like you end up doing all the work. You also need—and respond well to—positive acknowledgment about your work and accomplishments. You simply glow when others share with you how much they appreciate your insights, opinions, and advice!

At times, you can be very hard on yourself; hearing that you are fine just the way you are feels very reassuring. Since you are such a serious sort, it's very helpful if friends and colleagues listen to your concerns and worries, encourage you to lighten up, and show you how to gently laugh at yourself. Their levity helps to balance out your intense sincerity and focus.

It's key for you that others are fair and thoughtful because you certainly are—and you expect the same treatment in return. Finally, co-workers and friends will have an easier time obtaining your forgiveness if they are willing to sincerely apologize when they are inconsiderate.

If others could understand the motives behind your corrections and criticisms of them, they might empathize with you a bit more.

Your friends and family will need to look beyond your surface comments and recognize that your deepest desire is to help them. You have a big heart—you just have a hard time expressing it in a way that others can feel.

Admirable Qualities of a One

Wow, you can get a lot done! You are the dedicated, self-disciplined workhorse who everyone loves to have on the team. And you don't just work hard; you work to make the world a better place. Your high standards and ethics won't allow you to compromise in any way, and you have high expectations of colleagues and subordinates as well.

Employers love hiring you and will work hard to keep you happy since you have a tendency to become a workaholic in your zest for perfection. (After all, making everything perfect takes a long time!)

As the organized One, you are highly skilled. You consistently put together facts and data, have strong comprehension of material, make sound conclusions, and recommend wise courses of action. No other type is as dedicated, perseverant, responsible, and practical. As a result of your unique traits, you strive to be the best you can be and are able to bring out the best in others.

You are the advocate One, and everyone who champions a cause wants you on his or her side! You can visualize ideal situations and then work hard to make them a reality. And while you may tell yourself that you are logical and objective with regard to your choices in life, the truth is that you are an activist looking for some justification that will support what you feel called to do.

Pressures and Limitations

The flipside to these amazing skills is that you demand so much of yourself that you may sometimes feel tense, anxious, and overwrought. To put it simply, you take life too seriously. This leads to a feeling of being burdened with too much responsibility and wishing others would take on more work or make greater efforts. You feel a sense of disappointment with yourself and others when your lofty expectations aren't met.

> You may never be completely satisfied with the project, yourself, or your co-workers.

Everything has to be done according to your right way, and you may find yourself responding in a dogmatic, intolerant way to others' suggestions to do something differently. Of course, this won't win you any popularity contests at work!

When you don't receive ample praise and positive feedback, you may think that your work is not good enough, that you are never enough, or that others don't appreciate you fully; this can lead to a bit of obsessing about what you could have done differently. Be careful about negative self-talk since this can wear you down.

As Children

You may recall being very self-critical as a child, sometimes in anticipation of what others might tell you. This caused you to avoid activities where you thought you might not be able to excel or do them perfectly. You were very focused on living up to the expectations of the important adults in your life—your parents, teachers, community leaders, etc.

And you were highly responsible; even as a young child, you were always the one on whom people could count. You sometimes even took on the role of a parent.

Unfortunately, you may have missed out on feeling like a child and the simplistic joy of play.

Since you wanted to be seen as perfect, you held in what you perceived to be negative feelings, such as anger, disappointment, frustration, rage, and sadness. You may have felt that you would feel better inside if you were just perfect enough.

As Parents

Ones tend to be consistent and fair, and they teach their children about responsibility, ethics, and moral values. Firm discipline is also an integral part of your parenting approach. Your children know exactly what is expected of them—and what to expect if they don't comply with the house rules. The good news is that you encourage your children to be the best they can be and won't settle for anything less.

Tips for Living with Ones

In Love

As the perfectionist One, you have an amazing recall for facts and details; no kind gesture by the one you love (no matter how small) goes unnoticed. You melt when your partner arrives on time, remembers special dates, knows your friends' names, or takes the time to offer a proper introduction.

For someone to win you over, he or she will need to speak to you with kindness and respect, ask your permission before sharing your personal details with others, and check with you before agreeing to attend events together. It's important to you that you don't look foolish to others, and your ideal partner will recognize that.

Because you work hard working and are so responsible, you glow when your partner compliments you on your efforts, dependability, resourcefulness, and wisdom.

> Your mate should know that you are not so generous with compliments in return.

Your ideal mate will spend time on self-improvement and building character. It would be wise not to flaunt any achievements to you. If he or she makes a mistake (as we all will now and then), your partner will need to admit the error of his or her ways immediately in order to prevent you from building up anger and resentment.

Look for someone who can help you lighten up and who knows how to laugh and see the lighter side of life. This will balance out your serious nature and bring a sense of fun to your relationship. Humour helps you stop worrying. As a consistent One, you tend to repeat known behaviours; finding a mate who likes to try new things would be a good balance for your tendency for routine.

Your partner will want to avoid power struggles with you because Ones need to be right. One great way to resolve any potential conflict is for you both to acknowledge that there are at least two right ways of doing anything!

It will be important for your partner to have his or her own interests to pursue independently since you tend to work long hours and don't need as much time together as they might want.

In your perfect relationship, you will want clearly defined guidelines for responsibilities (paying bills, housekeeping, yard work, errands), and you will spend a great deal of time reflecting on what you are learning from your connection.

> Your ethical nature will have you delving into the idea of a
> "right relationship" with another.

Forewarn your mate that you tend to generalize when things go sour. If you begin to feel that the relationship isn't working out well, you may consider calling it off entirely. This is a result of your black-or-white thinking and can sneak up on a partner who hasn't been prepared for your quick change of mind.

One last word of caution: sometimes when you are having a great time together, you may feel a sense of guilt rising. For you, pleasure can trigger feelings of anxiety because you are the type to worry that bad things may happen if you're having too much fun.

The good news is that once you are committed and sure that this is the right relationship for you, you will dig in and set up house. You are an extremely loyal One and will place great value on having a family.

In the Workplace

At work, as at home, you like to have things spelled out: guidelines, policies, schedules, timelines, back-up plans, clear accountability, etc. To you, loopholes are black holes and can be quite traumatizing. You are the master of detail and are great at keeping track of all the things that others find bothersome and pesky. Be careful that your energy isn't completely spent on all those details, leaving none for the actual project.

Watch that you don't get too bogged down in all the details; you may have a hard time seeing the bigger picture and proposing broad solutions. You also want to learn to delegate effectively since your natural inclination is to do it yourself so it gets done right.

You are the practical One, and you have the uncanny ability to take abstract approaches and turn them into step-by-step procedures. You prefer actions to feelings; you're a doer and are all business. You tend to spend more time and energy on the work at-hand than on building relationships or rapport with your co-workers.

When working with others, you value an ethical nature—character is important to you, and you look for evidence of it in self-discipline, manners, appearances, and respectfulness. You also are keenly aware of the qualifications on resumes, work records, and attendance records.

> Watch out for your tendency to keep score!

You automatically note what others are doing, right or wrong, and like to air the good news *and* your complaints about them. You also don't want to be blamed for the mistakes of others. Sometimes this means you'll work alone instead of risking error being unjustly assigned to you.

You truly are afraid to be wrong or make mistakes, and you are apt to get into power struggles over who's to blame, who's right, who was at fault, and the reason behind the error.

You will feel most secure in a formal role where you can receive respect through your position and authority. Your tendency is to compare your work efforts to those of others. If you're around a hard-working group, you will work hard too. If you're around a bunch of goof-offs, you may join them instead of feeling put-upon as the only one left working.

Your devotion is to work for the sake of work, and you take pleasure in a job well done. You will work hard for the right cause, an inspired leader, a capable team, or the good of mankind.

> As a noble One, you really want to make the world a better place.

Be aware that you have a knack for making your own feelings of personal entitlement all about the good cause when it's really more about what you need to feel better about yourself. You may feel that you deserve to be paid more because you "do good work."

As a manager, you may find it hard to delegate responsibility because you worry that others won't do something correctly—or it won't be done your way (the right way). One of your strengths as a manager is being a strong advocate for anyone who works under a disadvantage or who makes concerted efforts to improve himself or herself.

11

You also tend to avoid taking risks because you think risks lead to mistakes. Your default mode is to wait if you're unsure and not take chances. In some organizations, this may be seen as a positive trait; in others, it can prove to be a job-ender.

You enjoy being recognized for your contributions; however, you will not ask for a raise or promotion. You feel that others should notice your efforts; if they don't, you may find yourself feeling resentment that can spill over into your daily work. Be careful not to allow hurt feelings to affect how you view others; you may be more prone to finding faults with them when you feel unappreciated.

Self-Preservation Measures

As the self-controlled One, you are always worrying about something: finances, job security, what's going wrong with the world, or even what you'll prepare for dinner. Changes to your routine make you anxious, and you may stay in an unsatisfying or inappropriate job for years instead of facing the anxiety and fear of looking for something more fulfilling.

> Your black-and-white-thinking puts a lot of pressure on you.

You feel as if one mistake could ruin everything you've worked so hard to build—this can cause you to procrastinate if you become frozen from the fear of doing something wrong.

You often imagine that someone is watching your every move and scrutinizing your work and decisions. You may frequently compare yourself to others, correct yourself, apologize unnecessarily, or feel that you should apologize (even when you won't say anything).

The dark side of your attention to detail is that you can overanalyse every minute detail in an attempt to keep your life in order, controlled, and perfect. And when you have finished worrying about everything you can think of in your world, you turn your worrying mind to your loved ones and their safety.

In Relationships

As the insecure and jealous One, you tend to be overly possessive of your mate. You harbour fears that you will be rejected for a more attractive or perfect specimen; as a result, you obsessively compare yourself to others.

Things that your partner says to compliment another, you will interpret as an affront to you. For example, your partner says, "She's a great dresser," but you hear, "You are not a good dresser." Because of your inclination to skew the interpretation of things, you build up a lot of negative feelings (embarrassment, anger, resentment, jealousy, indignation, and shame). You may act overly positive or enthusiastic to mask your true feelings (which you deem to be improper or unacceptable).

If your partner or a friend receives accolades or honours that you feel weren't earned—or you feel you are more deserving of your friend's promotion—you will well up with indignation and anger.

> The intensity of your emotions may overwhelm you, but you will not reveal your true feelings to others.

You interpret anger (and other negative emotions) as character flaws; you'll repress your feelings and keep them bottled up inside where they will eat away at you.

You enjoy the intensity of being fully committed and passionately engaged with another, and you will encourage your partner to meet your lofty standards and expectations in an effort to make your relationship (and mate) better.

Socially

As the unyielding One, you can defend something adamantly and dig your feet in to the point where you annoy and irritate others. You don't understand why they are put off since you have spent so much time and careful deliberation in coming to your conclusion and forming your opinion. You see no reason to change your mind; in matters of conscience, you will not agree to anything less than your highest principles.

In other cases, you may want to speak up and help champion reform efforts, but instead you quietly simmer and stew in an attempt to keep from rocking the boat. At these times, you have decided that getting along is more important than sharing your values with others.

You believe in working cooperatively, but when people don't meet your high standards, you feel the need to correct them and teach them the right way (your way). Unfortunately, they don't take very kindly to your criticism—and neither would you! Try to catch yourself before you correct others.

Realize that you are not the "manager of the universe," and it's not up to you to ensure that everyone else does his or her job according to your standards.

You are drawn to groups that espouse high ideals, but you tend to throw yourself in too much. You end up overworking yourself and feeling resentful because others aren't contributing as much or as well as you are. In the end, you may feel the need to leave the group in order to feel better.

One's worldview: The world is imperfect, yet I continue to work towards self-improvement and perfection.

Core Issues for Ones

You have lost your sense of peace and serenity and will not feel complete until you reclaim it. You focus your attention on the external environment, looking to correct all the wrongs of the world, and you lose sight of the fact that you are rejecting yourself as flawed, imperfect, unworthy, and "not enough."

You're willing to work hard and sacrifice for your lofty goals, but when others don't work just as hard, you feel self-righteous, rigid, irritable, and judgmental.

When you recognize that life is perfect in its imperfection—and that everything is just fine exactly the way it is—then you will know peace. And once you feel peaceful inside and have stopped the war on yourself, people will warm up to you, your relationships will be stronger and more meaningful, and you will actually feel carefree and able to have fun!

Sample Questions

- Was I aware of where my energy and attention were placed today?
- If I reacted too quickly (without thinking), was I able to redirect my awareness and recognize my overreaction?
- Have I been judging or criticizing myself today?
- Did I feel judged or criticized by others today?

- What has my self-talk been like? Negative? Neutral? More supportive?
- Did I feel resentful at all today? If so, what was it about?
- Did I see situations as good or bad or right or wrong—or was I able to see the grey areas?
- What is one thing I said to someone today that could have been interpreted as criticism?
- How can I rephrase that next time so it sounds more like a caring suggestion?
- What did I worry about today? A year from now, will that still be important?

The Core of Healing

- Recognize that judgment and rightness are not part of the natural order of things.
- Have compassion for yourself and for others.
- Interrupt and stop the internal critic; speak kindly to yourself.
- Learn to relax, have fun, play, and see yourself as acceptable and okay the way you are.
- Make mistakes and live to tell about them!
- Stop comparing yourself to others—and others to you. See each person as a unique individual.
- Know that you are worthy just for being you—without having to do anything to earn it.
- Love yourself.

Affirming Change

Affirmations, when used properly, are powerful tools for change. Affirmations are designed to speak directly to the subconscious mind and effect change on a level much deeper than your rational or conscious thoughts.

To use affirmations effectively, it's important to feel what you're saying and accept it as valid and real. Therefore, it's helpful to begin with an affirmation that allows you to release old beliefs and any thoughts that are no longer serving you. This is followed by a positive affirmation that brings in a new idea.

Begin by saying both affirmations. Once you feel comfortable saying the second affirmation, you can drop the first one and just use the second one:

- I release the need to judge and hold myself and others to impossible standards. I let go of my need to control and the belief that it is up to me to fix everything.
- I now choose to be gentle and forgiving of myself and others. I believe in miracles and allow them to unfold for me.

Opportunities for Growth

As a dedicated One, begin to question your harsh internal standards and requirements. Question your rules and policies for living—and begin to accept that good enough is acceptable (rather than striving for perfection).

> Notice when you are feeling compulsive or when doing takes over.

Schedule time for yourself to just be so that you can begin to identify your true priorities in life. And when you do take time to self-reflect, be careful not to interpret your areas for growth as areas where you've been wrong or failed at something. Begin to be gentle with yourself.

Give yourself a reality check. When you are worried that others are criticizing or judging you, check it out with them and find out what they're really thinking. You may be pleasantly surprised! Using your skill with details to face the facts will help you eliminate unnecessary worries.

Catch yourself when you begin to think that there is only one right way; this type of thinking limits your options and keeps you from reaching fair compromises.

> Begin to pay attention to the validity of others' values and ethics.

Forgive real and perceived errors in yourself and others—adopt a "that was then, this is now" attitude. Start to observe and change your habit of using *should* statements ... replace these with *I want* statements that affirm your desires and priorities.

Express your negative feelings as they occur. Find ways to do this that are not offensive to others—but still get your point across. Recognize that these feelings are indicators of your real wishes and desires. For example, if you are thinking, *It's not fair that he got a promotion without working hard,* you may be feeling unappreciated for your efforts. Perhaps it's time for you to approach your boss about a raise or a promotion.

If you are not expressing your feelings in a healthy way, you may have a tendency to use polite words in a sharp tone or to smile while maintaining a rigid body. In other words, you will convey your feelings one way or the other; focus on expressing them in appropriate ways that can help you meet your needs. As you begin to get in touch with your feelings, you may find that they are unruly and messy.

Seeking professional help or keeping a journal may prove beneficial to you. You will come to realize that being human is a messy business—and feelings are an integral part of the experience.

Your greatest weakness is unexpressed anger or rage. You are easily offended by others' actions—even when their actions are in keeping with their values. Remember that not everyone lives by your value system. Try to see that your anger is hurting you, and it is alienating you from having meaningful connections with others. In the long run, it may cause physical problems such as ulcers, high blood pressure, or heart attacks.

Learn what makes you happy and start to ask for the things that please you. Tell your partner and friends what little gestures touch your heart and make you feel seen and valued.

Find some time for yourself—time to relax without feeling that you need to accomplish something. Recognize that the world will continue to spin on its axis even if you take a day off! And make an effort to get away on weekends and vacations.

> One who is out of his or her routine environment can finally relax and enjoy life.

You have much to share with others and are a wonderful teacher, but don't expect others to change immediately. Since they may have different learning styles, personalities, and ways of perceiving things, give them the space they need to grow and learn at their own paces. Have patience and know that your words and actions model principled behaviour and are more impactful than any preaching could be.

Learn to let go of your role as manager of the universe—the only person who suffers from your intense irritations with others' shortcomings is you. And along that same line, soften up on yourself. Your harsh, demanding pushing of yourself doesn't serve you well.

> You will respond better to a gentler, more encouraging approach.

Stages of Evolution

For every personality type, there are opportunities to live from several different stages of growth, depending on whether you are reflective and interested in growing or are happy with the status quo. In addition, not everyone who is a One will have every trait or quality described here. Some will have traces of a characteristic, and others will see that same characteristic in abundance. A general overview of each stage is followed by a more detailed description.

Deteriorating

Dogmatic, punishing, self-righteous, resentful, critical, obsessive, unable to adapt, strongly opinionated, ornery, workaholic, perfectionist, angry, rageful, over reactive, scared being condemned, defensive, can't be seen as wrong, have all the answers, self-loathing, judgmental

You become resentful, moody, and isolated when you realize that others don't take your high ideals seriously. The sense of obligation to do everything—because others simply won't do things as well or as quickly—helps your resentment grow. You begin to feel misunderstood and may withdraw to lick your wounds and figure out your feelings.

If you live with prolonged stress, you may become disillusioned with life, your family, your job, your co-workers, and yourself. This can lead to depression or behaviours that offer an escape for you—despite the fact that they are clearly not in line with your values. Unfortunately, you'll find little relief because you will begin to feel guilty about the indulgences.

At your worst, your obsession with perfection can cause you to be cruel and downright malicious towards others, punishing them for perceived errors. If you remain in this state for too long, it can lead to a nervous breakdown and possibly even a suicide attempt.

Status Quo

Orderly, organized, practical, critical, controlling, desire to fix everything, know-it-all, inflexible, tense, rigid, distant, overly analytical, truth-seeking, need to be right, hard working, righteous, feeling unworthy, striving for perfection, lots of integrity, always working to improve

You desire a safe environment; when you feel secure, you are willing to let your hair down a bit and be less inhibited. You're also able to access and express your emotions more readily when you feel safe.

> You even have an impulsive, adventurous side to you. (Who knew?)

You may take the expression of your feelings a bit too far and become demanding, selfish, and needy. When stressed, you may lose the ability to focus and feel as if your energy is scattered in too many directions at once. As a result, you have a tendency to look for something to distract you so that you won't feel overwhelmed by all the responsibilities and obligations.

You can be highly critical of yourself and others and may express strong opinions as facts. You can feel as if only you know the truth and use this to justify your actions. Be careful not to badger others in an attempt to get them to live by your standards. At your worst, you can be scolding and abrasive, preaching to people from a moral high ground that only you see.

You may grow dissatisfied with reality and see yourself as a lofty idealist, a crusader, or an activist who will save the world from itself. This is all in an effort to change the world to the way you know it should be.

> You'll often become a workaholic in your efforts to reform everyone and everything.

The Alarm

As the passionate crusader, you become aware of a feeling of obligation and responsibility to fix absolutely everything. Once you recognize this and the silliness of it, you allow yourself to let go a little. When you learn to relax your grip on controlling and fixing everything to your impossible standards, you begin to be gentler to yourself. You can commit to grow in a way that allows you to accept yourself and others and to develop a genuine tolerance for the way things are.

Evolving

Principled, ethical, idealistic, conscientious, good, realistic, moral, truth-seeking, like to do the right thing, interested in helping others grow, practical, good with details, hard worker, always pursuing self-improvement, responsible

You have strong convictions balanced with a conscientious approach to others. You recognize that your deep sense of right and wrong is meaningful to you—but not to everyone else. You are highly principled and choose to be fair and just in your treatment of situations and people, including yourself.

You are rational, reasonable, and moderate in your approach to life. You recognize the limits of your responsibilities, live with integrity, and know your higher purpose—making you a fantastic teacher, advocate, or mentor.

On Your Spiritual Path

High integrity, compassionate, kind to self and others, tolerant, playful, able to relax, disciplined, just, advocate, accepting of self and others, able to recognize individuality of others, open to other ways of doing things, recognize the perfection in imperfection, filled with self-love

Once you've learned to give yourself (and others) some slack, you will experience a feeling of freedom and joy with life.

> You can be spontaneous, adventurous, light-hearted, expressive, and fun.

You no longer see the world as yours to fix; instead, you have come to a place of balance and understand personal choice, personal freedom, and how to live with acceptance, tolerance, and love for yourself and others. Life feels abundant and wonderful now!

You have thrown away your list of "shoulds" and "have-tos'" and are more readily in touch with your creativity, dreams, and realistic ideals. You are now open to the possibilities that exist throughout life, and you know that you don't have the answers for anyone except yourself.

Because you are more emotionally expressive, light-hearted, and flexible, people are drawn to you and can easily hear your ideas and opinions. You feel more connected to people and have deeper relationships than you ever imagined were possible.

You no longer feel resentful, and you live from a place of gratitude for everything that shows up in life. You accept what is and live without expectations of yourself or others. You have become amazingly wise and insightful, and you trust your knowing about what the right course of action is in any given moment. You inspire others by speaking your truth in a caring and considerate way.

Type One: The Instigator

As the instigator of great things, you have a vision of balance and completion—along with a strong desire to make the world a better place. Your dedication, perseverance, and hard work are laudable. When you are at your best, you are disciplined, idealistic, ethical, principled, fair, conscientious, realistic, and tolerant.

> Ones can be an employer's dream come true.

Be aware that your Achilles' heel is your unwillingness to express your anger and get your needs met. You struggle to find the balance between rigidity and sensitivity, between perfection and vulnerability.

You are addicted to perfection and have a tendency towards compulsive behaviours. You set high internal standards for yourself and beat yourself up over perceived mistakes. You also can be highly critical of others, which creates a barrier to developing deep connections.

But do not worry—it is possible for you to achieve a sense of serenity with the world, to feel confident in your abilities, and to learn to express your feelings appropriately.

When you learn to accept others as they are, recognize that not everyone follows the same set of values that you do, and feel peaceful in the world, you will be ready to live at your highest potential. You will come to the realization that we are all one with each other—and that everything is perfect the way it is.

This feeling of acceptance, this bird's-eye view, helps you see that there are many right answers to any given situation or question. When you recognize the perfection in human imperfection, you will open yourself up to a larger version of self—the compassionate One.

You will be well on your way to instigating your wonderful vision of a better world!

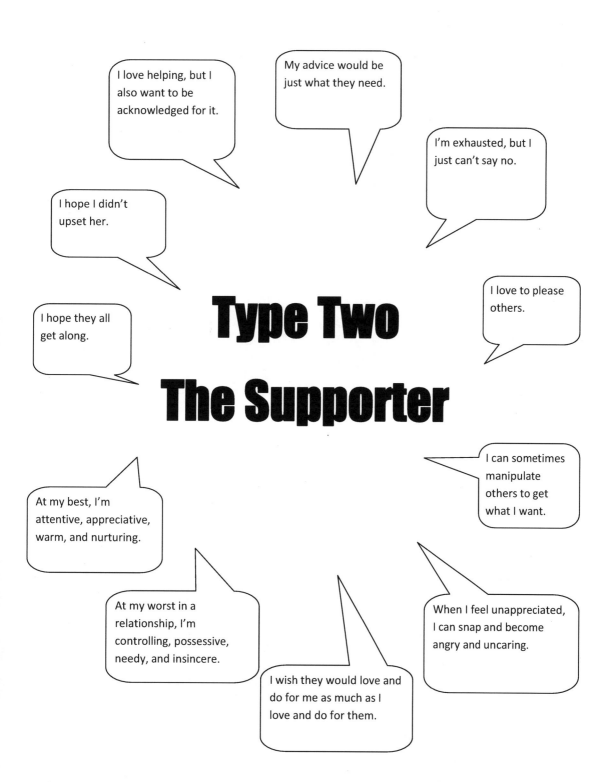

2

Type Two—The Supporter

As Type Two (the Supporter), you are affectionate, caring, and generous—and you love to please others. You enjoy it when people depend on you and need your help. You love to be loved, but your secret fear is that you aren't really loveable.

You enjoy being the centre of attention, and you are adept at creating connections with powerful people who can benefit you or your agenda. And while you enjoy associating with people of status or privilege, you are somewhat reticent to step into the limelight. This is most likely due to an underlying fear of failure.

You follow your strong intuition when learning new things, and are open to others' ideas, although sometimes you can be too easily influenced. You make friends easily and seek out a love connection, but you are secretly afraid of true intimacy and may take steps to ensure that it doesn't occur.

> At your best, you are warm, engaging, and always giving to others.

You make people feel welcome and comfortable, and you are very helpful and generous. You enjoy identifying others' needs through your keen intuition—and then meeting their needs, even when you haven't been asked.

Be careful of your tendency to deny your own needs; this will only end up with you playing the hysterical martyr role. In matters of the heart, you would be wise to be open and honest with your partner. Avoid your baser nature that would have you manipulate, possess, or use a mate.

As the romantic Two, you believe deeply in the power of love—and you see love as the source of all good things. In some ways, you're correct, but love is a much deeper and broader construct that what some Twos think it is. You think of love as feeling good, being of service to another, and self-sacrifice. At its highest form, genuine love wants only what is best for the other—even if it means you aren't in his or her life anymore.

Your type runs the gamut from the angelic giver to the hateful devil—from unattached genuine love on one end of the spectrum, to the people pleaser at the mid-point, and the manipulative, obsessive stalker on the other end of the spectrum.

But when you learn who you really are, are willing to identify your needs, and can share yourself with the world, you can move from a place of needing to align with powerful people to a feeling of personal strength and confidence as you share your generous caring nature with the world.

In a Positive, Healthy State

Your desire to be loved drives you to help others and make their lives better; in turn, they reciprocate by caring about you and feeling grateful and appreciative of you. This satisfies your need to be loved and helps you maintain balance in life.

> At your best, you are a selfless angel who blesses others' lives with
> your generosity and kindness.

You are a good listener, and your highly refined intuitive nature enables you to tune in to others' needs—sometimes better than they can! This is what makes you the ideal right arm to a successful, busy person. They know that they can count on you to know what they need and attend to it before they can even articulate it or ask for your assistance!

You go for what you want in life, and you have perfected your ability to attract people and events that benefit you. Having mastered the art of flattery, you use this skill to create rapport with those who might benefit you. Be careful not to lose yourself in your zeal to be exactly what is needed in each situation.

As the giving Two, you want nothing more than to be perceived as appealing, thoughtful, and heartfelt—and you want to be needed. Your self-perception is that of a nurturing, caring, approachable person.

You wish more people recognized your efforts as empathetic, altruistic, and noble.

You have the ability to make people feel comfortable around you, and others enjoy your warm company. Creating mutual trust and affinity with others comes naturally to you. You have a strong desire to be of service, but you need to be cautious about not overlooking your own needs in your efforts to please others.

In order to live your best life, you will want to learn more about yourself and your personal strengths, learn to identify your needs and find ways to meet them, and only give to others when it's a heartfelt desire (not because you want to impress them, get noticed, or be loved in return).

When you can live from a place of genuine caring and let go of your expectations about what you'll get from people, you will find that life can be peaceful and enjoyable, and you'll know what it feels like to love and be loved.

In a Detrimental, Unhealthy State

When you are out of balance, your fear of not being loved can cause you to feel resentment, and it can drive you to try to manipulate others into loving you. Unfortunately, this causes people to pull back from you and offer you less love, which creates greater distress for you as you see your worst fear being realized. If this cycle is not interrupted, it will continue in a downward spiral, leaving you feeling lost and alone, unloved and unseen. At your lowest point, you even have the potential to stalk your beloved target.

Your intense desire to feel love can cause you to act out in some less-than-ideal ways. Be aware of your baser nature that would allow you to abuse food or over-the-counter medications as a way of numbing your pain. Bingeing on sweets and excess carbohydrates, overeating because you're starved for love, and being a hypochondriac in order to obtain sympathy are all techniques that the love-starved Two has been known to use.

Your downfall is your pride; you believe that you see clearly what others' needs are.

Unfortunately, you give with strings attached! By helping people when they haven't even asked for your help, you attempt to create indebtedness. As a result, others may perceive you as bossy or manipulative, nosey, or intrusive.

And while you are a dependable, awesome number Two to powerful people, if you're not careful, your continual submission to another will cause you to identify too much with them. This can lead you to a loss of your sense of self, not knowing who you are anymore, and may even leave you in a state of depression. At other times, you may find yourself acting out hysterically and demanding your share of attention.

One final word of caution: you have the uncanny ability to be a chameleon, meaning you can adapt yourself to be whatever others need you to be (even when they haven't actually stated their needs). And while this might please the other person in the short-term, it will have dire consequences for you both in the long run. They will wake up one day to realize you are not who you pretended to be—and they will wonder who they are living with! If your loved one pulls away from you, you could easily lose your sense of self, give up your personal freedom and choices, and become aggressive.

Tips for Getting Along with Twos

You might want to share some important points with close friends, family, and those with whom you work closely. These ideas may help others understand you better and teach them how best to interact with the people-pleasing Two.

It's important to you that people appreciate you and are specific with praise and compliments. If they do offer criticism, you will respond best if it's very gentle and encouraging.

> Your warm, concerned, nurturing nature makes you especially sensitive to other people's opinions and comments.

As a generous Two, you need friends and family to take an active interest in your problems— even when you try to turn the attention back towards them. And you want your closest friends and significant other to let you know how special you are and how much they value you. It's important to you to share fun times with others and to feel reassured that they enjoy spending time with you.

You love nothing better than to be perceived as a special friend—someone who goes out of your way, can be counted on day or night, and will give the shirt off your back. And you don't mind doing all of this, as long as you receive enough validation, admiration, and gratitude from the recipients.

While you may consciously think the reason you are so generous with your time and energy is because of your loving nature, the truth is that you are secretly feeling needy and vulnerable. You feel as if you have to earn love from others. As a result, you continually give, give, give to avoid intense loneliness. Your friends and loved ones can make you happiest by spending time with you, enjoying your company, and not letting you do everything for them.

In your most intimate relationship, you will want to be reassured that you are interesting to your lover and will need to hear frequently how much you are loved. They can never tell you enough how attractive you are and how glad they are to be with you!

Admirable Qualities of a Two

As the connected Two, you find it easy to relate to people and make new friends. In fact, this is one of your gifts! Your sensitive, warm, generous ways and keen intuition make you an easy person to be around; you are always tuned into others' feelings and desires.

This emotional intelligence allows you to create rapport even with difficult people. You know exactly what to say to make others feel better.

> You have the natural ability to mirror others, which makes them feel comfortable with you immediately.

You are an enthusiastic, fun-loving friend who has a good sense of humour and knows how to enjoy life. You find satisfaction in knowing what people need and giving it to them in an effort to make their lives better. Who wouldn't want a friend like you?

In the workplace, you have a knack for knowing how to plan a project—even ones that involve large numbers of people and moving parts. You are able to identify various possible alternatives and clearly see how they may affect the outcome. When you combine those skills with your innate ability to solve complex problems, it makes you the go-to person for creating harmony and unity while getting the job done.

Pressures and Limitations

Intuitive Twos are so connected to what others are thinking and feeling, and so open to others' ideas and opinions, that you may be influenced too readily by outside input, causing you to allow an undue number of possibilities to cloud the picture.

It's very hard for the caring Two to say no to things, and this can result in you feeling drained from overdoing it, giving too much time and energy to others, and overextending yourself.

> You may also wake up one day to discover that you're not doing things that you really enjoy out of fear of feeling selfish.

You may experience low self-esteem and criticize yourself for not feeling as loving as you think you should feel. At times, you'll find yourself upset because others aren't as in tune with your feelings as you are with theirs. You can get overwrought from working so hard to be tactful, considerate, and thoughtful to others and completely suppress your own feelings and needs.

It can be frustrating to the entitled Two when others don't bestow you with the recognition, privilege, status, and power you feel you deserve. This can result in feeling humiliated, and you may feel the need to act out and demand that your presence is recognized.

As Children

You may recall feeling extremely sensitive to disapproval and criticism from adults or people of authority. You tried hard to please your parents by being as helpful and understanding as was possible for a child. You behaved in an outwardly compliant manner; at times, you may have acted coy, precocious, or dramatic in order to get the attention you craved.

You may have been popular with your peers—or tried to be popular with them—and might even have resorted to being the class clown or joker (if you're a more extroverted Two). On the other end of the spectrum, you may have become quiet, shy, and withdrawn (if you're a more introverted Two).

As Parents

Twos are good listeners and love their children unconditionally. You are encouraging, warm, demonstrative, and loving—and you tend to feel guilty if you're not!

> You are often quite playful with your kids and can prove to be a fiercely protective lion when they are in danger.

You tend to reflect on your parenting skills, wondering if you're doing it right, if you're giving enough, and if you have caused any irreparable damage to your children. This makes you a thoughtful parent—one who is willing to look at yourself in an effort to provide your children with the best possible upbringing.

Tips for Living with Twos

In Love

As the tender Two, you want to be the focus of your mate's life. You are happy when you feel independent and feel like you don't need your partner; at the same time, you want your partner to be dependent upon you.

Along this same line, you enjoy having power and control, but you do this in a way that appears to be compliant and giving, even subservient. As a result, your significant other will need to learn to recognize when you're being manipulative—some of your tactics include complaining and guilt trips—to get your mate to do your bidding.

Despite this outward appearance of control, you are very vulnerable inside and are afraid of rejection and loss with regard to your intimate relationship. You place a strong emphasis on this connection and would feel devastated if your partner were to leave you (you leaving them is another story!).

In order to succeed in love, the impetuous Two will need to learn how to be authentic. You will need to understand and share your true emotions—not just the melodramatic anger and hysteria that you use to demonstrate that your needs haven't been met. You may not know what you want or what you feel at first, but you can learn this skill with practice.

It will be important for your loved one to understand that you are prone to fits of superficial feelings, exhibited as a result of your insecurity and sensitivity. Your partner may see you break out in hysterical laughter, become hyperactive, or flirt inappropriately in an effort to cover your deep-seated feeling of inadequacy. You do this spontaneously as a coping technique to defuse the situation and chase away unwelcome feelings.

> You are very expressive and demonstrative when it comes to affection.

But you have a tendency to confuse sex or affection with love, thinking they are one and the same thing. While they may feel equal for you, they are not for most people. This is something you can learn—if you're open to it.

You probably haven't had much experience with true intimacy due to your difficulty accessing genuine emotions and being willing to be vulnerable. Typically, you've repressed your sexual and emotional feelings in order to attract a mate. You were more interested in pleasing your partner and meeting his or her needs than you were in identifying and meeting your own.

As you learn to access and express your authentic feelings and needs, you may experience some anger. It will no longer be okay with you to always please your mate, and this will be a challenge for you to reconcile.

Your partner can help you feel safer by allowing you to speak your mind, exert your personal will, and have your own ideas and interests. When your loved one gives you space to grow and become your true self, you will feel safe to blossom. Your partner can assist you by reassuring you that they still love you—even if you no longer rush to meet their every need.

The only potential problem is that as a feisty Two, you may start fighting for your independence. You may wake up one day and feel like you've wasted your time constantly catering to the needs of your partner—and having gone too long without having yours met.

> In the beginning of your relationship, your partner may feel as if they have won the jackpot by finding you!

After all, you cater to your partner's every whim and desire—without them having to ask for anything. You are affectionate and caring, intuitive to their wishes, and provide them with everything they could want or need. But you are a ticking time bomb. Until you learn to meet your own needs in a love relationship, it's just a matter of time before you realize you are tired of your partner not meeting your needs (never mind that you don't even know what they are, haven't shared them, and haven't asked for them to be met—that will become irrelevant when this all blows up).

A final word of caution: Twos like to get involved in relationships fraught with obstacles and challenges because these will prevent true intimacy from occurring. You also like to create love triangles; you may be involved with someone and secretly have someone else on the side. This helps you feel like you have a life raft, a place to jump to, should you want to bail out on your relationship on a moment's notice. But as you can probably guess, this also prevents you from ever experiencing real intimacy with your partner. You will need to let go of your desire for all these entanglements and obstacles if you wish to find a relationship with real staying power and a lasting love connection.

In the Workplace

You are the ideal right-hand person to powerful, important, busy people. You are the secretary who knows all the secrets, the power behind the throne, the assistant with all the influence, and the one who really knows how to get things from your boss. And you take your identity from this role from the person you work for. You attach to them and ride their coattails.

This doesn't mean you aren't talented! You simply won't step into the limelight; you'd rather be associated with someone who is important and successful and bask in the glow that surrounds him or her. The downside to this is you won't give the time of day to people you view as not worthwhile. You will support the office favourites without noticing the worker bees; even though you are one of them, you see yourself as superior and more aligned with the office stars.

> As a helpful Two, you have built-in radar that attunes you to what others want, and you believe you are the answer to their needs.

You will go out of your way to serve them, but it's not from solely altruistic motives. You enjoy the feeling that you get from being of service. You feel as if you are powerful enough to care for yourself—and anyone else who needs assistance.

You enjoy playing a central role in others' lives, feeling chosen and special, irreplaceable and needed. In your perception, *others* are needy and dependent. The truth is that you need to be appreciated, needed, and lavished with gratitude.

Co-workers and bosses should know that you are highly responsive to approval, positive feedback, and encouragement. You thrive on praise and rewards. The flipside of that is that you do not take constructive criticism well—and disapproval can crush you.

Be careful of becoming so externally focused on meeting others' needs that you literally don't know your own needs are going unmet. For example, if you feel compelled to offer someone a snack, perhaps you are the one who is actually hungry! You may believe that you must meet the needs of others *before* you deserve to have your own needs met.

You'll go to extra lengths to avoid appearing needy or disposable. You are so afraid of being ignored that you will avoid doing anything that might appear self-serving or off-putting.

> You have a secret desire to be the best, to be recognized and lauded, and this can come into conflict with your underlying need to please others.

You feel safe when you are pleasing the authorities or powers that be at your workplace, and you have a deep fear of opposing anyone in power by yourself. It would take being part of a large powerful group for you to consider any form of disagreement with management.

Because you are so in tune with what everyone wants and needs, you are also adept at knowing what's happening in the office and may even be the company grapevine, the party coordinator, or the one who organizes office gatherings and remembers the birthdays. You keep a close watch on what goes on and you know who's doing what and with whom.

The dark side to your generous nature is your pride. You secretly believe that you are the only one who can see what others need and provide it. In your mind, no one else is as good at being of service to others as you are!

As the industrious Two, you may not know why you chose the line of work that you're in. In many cases, it's because that career or industry is meaningful to someone you love, and you wanted to please them on some subconscious level. Because you're not aware of your own needs and desires, it is highly unlikely that you chose your career because it's something you enjoy doing.

> Trying to achieve personal fulfilment by meeting the needs of others is a theme in your life.

The truth is that giving more to others does not fulfil you; it simply cuts you off from your awareness of your own desires and wishes.

Self-Preservation Measures

As the nurturing Two, you are interested in helping people and always try to present a loving image. At the same time, you feel as if you deserve to be appreciated for all the things you've done for others. With this expectation of preferential treatment, if others do not treat you as lovingly as you treat them (i.e. with cards, gifts, and signs of appreciation for your devoted, loving, self-sacrificing nature), you can feel hurt, angry, and devastated.

You love to pamper yourself with indulgent treats, shopping trips, exotic vacations, and luxuries. You often will spend more than you need to, but you are able to rationalize it to yourself.

One way you've come up with to support your luxurious whims is to find a partner who will support you financially. In return, you will do whatever it takes to support your mate's goals in life. Helping your loved one achieve his or her full potential is gratifying to you and makes you feel important—it also helps you avoid stepping into your own greatness and risking possible failure.

Sometimes you feel young and needy, but you won't allow yourself to feel that way for long.

> You cover it up by acting helpful and strong, and you may even seek out a mate who will support you emotionally.

In Relationships

You are the seductive Two, and you go after what you want—whether it's a relationship or anything else in life. You are persistent and will reach out to others because you secretly fear that they will overlook you and forget about you if you don't.

You have perfected the art of luring in potential partners by altering your personality and dress, by learning about their likes and dislikes and feigning to have the same ones, by turning on your irresistible charm, and by paying rapt attention to a person's every word. You love the chase—but it's only after you've hooked them and reeled them in that you will decide if you like them or not!

You long to have a close relationship, but you know that you have lost yourself in them in the past. Because you spend so much time and effort intuiting your partner's needs and meeting them instantly, you have a hard time discerning your own needs, let alone meeting them. After a while in a relationship, you realize it's all about your partner, and you have practically disappeared.

In addition, you may choose inappropriate or unavailable people to connect with to keep from having to face your underlying fear of intimacy. When you decide on a mate, in many cases, you set out to improve them, change them, or bring out a different side of them.

> Despite your catering to his or her every whim, your partner may feel manipulated and moulded.

Socially

You enjoy making a difference in the lives of others and seek out important roles (like assisting the powerful leader), but you avoid work that makes you highly visible. Being centre stage would make you feel anxious and concerned that you might be embarrassed if you were to fail or fall short in some way.

You yearn to be recognized and valued for your loving qualities, your warmth, your friendliness, and for your skills and expertise. You try to obtain approval by being charming, competent, energetic, upbeat, positive, funny, and by entertaining in your home. The ultimate compliment for you is when someone says, "I couldn't have done it without you!" or "How could I ever live without you?" or "No one does it like you do."

You walk a fine line between wanting to support and encourage the success of others (like your partner and your boss) and resenting their success because you feel that you have contributed much of the work and are responsible for it. To be happy in this situation, your loved one or boss would need to lavish you with praise, recognition, and gifts so that you felt truly seen, valued, and appreciated—and then you would be happy for their success as well.

As the helper Two, your compulsive need to help others, whether they want it or not, may ultimately derail you. It is only when you acknowledge and satisfy your own needs and wishes that you will feel the freedom and fulfilment you seek.

> Two's worldview: People depend on me and need me.

Core Issues for Twos

You compulsively give and provide for others, and the price you pay is not having your own needs met, not feeling fulfilled, and not feeling appreciated enough. Your overdoing creates a continual deficit between you and those you care about—one that they can never fully reciprocate. Thus, your caring and generous nature has a baser side to it, and you can become possessive and manipulative.

Your self-perception is of someone who is virtuous, genuinely loving, considerate, and a real do-gooder. But others sometimes perceive you as needy, intrusive, nosey, a know-it-all, aggressive, manipulative, or domineering. As a result of this chasm between what you see and what others see, the good that you think you are doing for others may be quite harmful.

Sample Questions

- How has my focus and energy been spent this week? On others? On myself?
- What percentage of my attention has been placed externally? Internally?
- How quick was I to respond when I perceived my help was needed?
- Did I confirm that my help was indeed needed and wanted?
- How did I alter myself to fit what others seemed to need?
- Were there times when I felt indispensable? Did I take pride in that?
- When did I feel like I knew better than anyone else what was needed in a situation?
- Have I allowed myself to need anything from others?

- What have I done to take care of myself? To meet my needs?
- How have I balanced giving and receiving?

The Core of Healing

- Notice your own needs and wants; learn to identify them clearly.
- Begin to receive from others and be okay with it.
- Cultivate an independent, separate self-identity (not connected to a more powerful person).
- Build your own autonomy and sense of independence.

Affirming Change

Affirmations, when used properly, are powerful tools for change. Affirmations are designed to speak directly to the subconscious mind and effect change on a level much deeper than your rational or conscious thoughts.

To use affirmations effectively, it's important to feel what you're saying and accept it as valid and real. Therefore, it's helpful to begin with an affirmation that allows you to release old beliefs and any thoughts that are no longer serving you. This is followed by a positive affirmation that brings in a new idea.

Begin by saying both affirmations. Once you feel comfortable saying the second affirmation, you can drop the first one and just use the second one:

- I release my need to be needed, the feelings of being victimized, and that others owe me for what I have done for them.
- I now affirm that I can love and do things for others unconditionally and without any expectations. I am good enough. I am loveable. I allow my heart to fill with joy and love. I am the power in my world.

Opportunities for Growth

As a giving Two, begin to recognize your own needs instead of spending all your time and energy identifying and meeting the needs of everyone else. One way to do this is to discover the core part of you, your unchanging essence, and live from that steady, consistent place instead of being the chameleon that changes to match each situation.

Another helpful technique is to allow your definition of caring to encompass both caring for others and caring for yourself—it doesn't have to be "either or." In fact, you can best care for others once you have met your own needs first.

> Your generous nature is laudable, but it's important to give with the right motives.

Giving to get something or to obtain someone's love or respect will not help you feel loved. Instead, learn to tune in to your underlying motive and only give when it comes from your heart without expecting anything in return. That is when you will know the true feeling of generosity.

If you don't pay attention to this, the martyr-like Two is in real danger of falling into unconscious, co-dependent patterns with your partner. This will result in never getting what you really want from the relationship or from life.

Along this same line, learn to become a good receiver and allow others to give to you for a change and graciously accept their help, gifts, and love. Over-giving can lead you to exhaustion, resentment, anger, not taking care of yourself, and a desire to escape.

And when you give, try not to tell everyone about it. They will notice and be appreciative or they won't be; reminding them of your good deeds will not satisfy anyone and may even harm your relationships.

> Learn to discern when people want your help.

You can do this very simply by asking them if they would like your help. If they don't need or want it, understand that this is not a rejection of you, your skills, or your loving nature. It is just that they don't need help.

Likewise, when you are dating, do not try to get someone to love you by giving gifts or unwarranted compliments. And on the flipside of this, if they don't respond the way you'd like them to, don't sharply withdraw your assistance. Neither of these behaviours will help you be seen or valued for who you really are. What they will do is leave you alone, without a partner, and wondering what happened.

Develop the awareness that real intimacy and abiding love can only be achieved if you truly love yourself first. You can't fake it with yourself and then expect to have a deep connection with another. Learn to acknowledge your underlying feelings, even when you deem them messy or unpleasant, and begin to express your feelings in healthy ways, making yourself heard.

Making these changes will provide you with a great opportunity to feel and know your own true worth. Your value is not connected to how much or how often you give; instead, it is based on who you are at your core. You are an amazing, loving human being—even when you're not doing things for others. Let go of the need to see yourself as indispensable or as everyone's best friend; these roles take a toll on you and will ultimately leave you feeling empty, angry, and possibly physically ill.

Let's consider the analogy of the airplane safety guidelines that instruct you to put on your oxygen mask before taking care of others. This is a good rule of thumb for you: be sure to take care of your needs first, ensuring you get sufficient rest and meeting your physical and emotional needs, before you attend to the needs of others. This is not selfish behaviour—it is just common sense.

> If you don't take care of yourself first, you will have nothing left to give to others.

When you find you are flattering someone or altering your behaviour to please them, stop for a moment and check in with yourself. Are you being sincere or are you trying to manipulate the situation? Recognize that your desires to flatter another to obtain approval are signs of your own rising anxiety and inner turmoil. Realize that exaggerated displays of emotion on your part typically mask your true feelings of inadequacy and fear of not being loved.

Notice your pride and how it rises and falls, inflates and deflates. Watch how when it inflates it does so as a result of you obtaining external approval and shifting blame onto others. Watch how when it deflates it's connected to not receiving enough appreciation or gratitude. By noticing, without judging yourself, you will become more in tune with your emotions and better able to express your real feelings safely in the future.

Stages of Evolution

For every personality type, there are opportunities to live from several different stages of growth, depending on whether you are reflective and interested in growing or are happy with the status quo. In addition, not everyone who is a Two will have every trait or quality described here. Some will have traces of a characteristic, and others will see that same characteristic in abundance. A general overview of each stage is followed by a more detailed description.

Deteriorating

Hostile, needy, dependent in an unhealthy way, manipulative, possessive, false flatterer, ingratiating, dominating, filled with pride, invasive, bossy, nosey, martyr, repressive, out of touch with self, false, feel like a victim, resentful, angry, overly dramatic, self-destructive, egocentric, controlling, attention-seeking, confrontational, temperamental, remorseless, apathetic

As the always-being-of-service Two, you have the potential to feel like a martyr or a victim, or both. When your many gestures of help and self-sacrifice go underappreciated or ignored, you may reach a breaking point, a place of intense stress, where you begin to vent and express all those suppressed feelings of anger, resentment, and injustice.

At this point, you cannot contain yourself for a minute longer—and your well-controlled emotional dam bursts. You can't maintain your loving attitude anymore. You feel overlooked, unseen, and taken for granted. You may act out by attempting to control the situation, becoming dominating and bossy, or by telling everyone what to do, how to do it, and when.

You have the potential to step out of (what most would perceive as) your character—to become an uncaring, apathetic, insensitive person who can be aggressive, confrontational, angry, throwing temper tantrums, threatening to withdraw your assistance from the project, etc.

> At this point, it is clear that you weren't giving from your heart, but rather from a deep-seated need to feel loved, needed, and included.

Status Quo

Complimentary, generous, indispensable, externally focused, positive, appreciative, expressive, helpful, friendly, outgoing, tuned in to others' needs, intuitive, overly intimate, intrusive, meddling, give with strings attached, speak with double meanings, possessive, co-dependent, extremely touchy, easily hurt, self-indulgent

When you are with trusted friends or your partner, you may find yourself opening up and sharing more of your real feelings. You begin to be honest about your baser impulses because you're simply tired of keeping up the charade that you are selfless and above being hurt by others' insensitive actions.

You may become moody, emotional, focused more on yourself, temperamental, self-doubting, and less bubbly and helpful. At times like these, you are extremely sensitive and may be hurt easily by comments that normally would be viewed as harmless.

You may also find yourself indulging—eating more sweets and pastries, taking up smoking, drinking more than usual—in an effort to appease your wounded ego for the innumerable sacrifices you've made for others.

The Alarm

As the ever-giving Two, you wake-up and realize that you've had it all wrong! You don't have to seek out others and intuit their needs and meet them before people even know you exist. In order to experience love from others, you need to do the opposite: love yourself and meet your needs. When others express their needs to you, ask if they would appreciate your help.

Evolving

Giving, generous, helpful, considerate, thoughtful, loving, caring, intuitive, forthright, expressive, in touch with emotions, aware of own needs, accepting of self and others, honest, sense of humour, see self objectively, supportive, nurturing, sensitive, creative

When you are healthy, your love is truly heartfelt and you genuinely desire to help others. You have learned to balance this with your ability to recognize and attend to your own needs and wants, making you feel harmonious and fulfilled.

> Your giving comes from a place of caring—rather than a place of needing to be noticed or appreciated.

You become aware of how you've mistreated others in the past, all in the name of selfless generosity, and you recognize how much you've ultimately deceived yourself about your motives and drives.

Now when you give, it's because you care and want to be of service for all the right reasons. You no longer help when you're not asked or invited to. You honour the independent spirit in others and know that they are fully capable of requesting help if they need it.

You are now able to really see your partner and want what's best for them—even if it means spending time apart from each other. You are feeling whole and connected in your relationships and are a much better friend now.

On Your Spiritual Path

Humble, unconditionally loving, accepting, compassionate, authentic, aware, conscious, balanced, capable of great intimacy, connected, fulfilled, nurturing, tender, affectionate, sympathetic, warm, concerned

You feel total acceptance for yourself and others, and you are able to tolerate situations where your help is not needed or wanted.

> You no longer reject aspects of yourself and have integrated your baser feelings as valuable parts of the whole of who you are.

You understand now, in hindsight, that your extensive giving was really a form of taking. You were giving, not from an altruistic place, but from a place of wanting something in return. You used to give with an agenda, an expectation, but that is not true now.

You are selfless in the truest sense of the word; you are a truly altruistic giver who can serve freely without any expectation of even a thank you in return. Having become deeply humble, you now give unconditionally to yourself and others, and you see it as a privilege to do so.

Even negative feelings that you may have are held with knowing and compassion; you are honest with yourself and accept your own humanity and emotions. You see yourself objectively through the balanced eyes of love.

Supporting others is easy for you, and you do this from a place of fullness instead of lack. You are more intimate in your closest relationships and have much deeper connections with friends. You have become the authentic self: caring, sensitive, creative, and expressive!

Type Two: The Supporter

You are a loving, warm, generous person who will go out of your way to help others and make a difference in their lives. You are friendly and fun, organized and efficient, skilful and highly competent. In addition, you have highly refined intuitive abilities and are able to know what others are thinking and feeling even before they do!

The drawback to the giving Two is your compulsive need to be of service, your desire to manipulate others to get what you want, your knack for adapting to any situation and becoming whatever another person wants you to be, and your reluctance to identify and fulfil your own needs and desires.

The good news is that you are valuable and have so much to offer the world—
all you have to do is learn about yourself.

Begin to recognize who you really are and become consistent in being yourself in all different types of situations—even when it's not convenient for others. By doing so, you will start to develop an appropriate sense of self-value and an understanding of your strengths and wonderful qualities, balanced with a deep respect and awareness of your limitations and areas for growth. In other words, you will become humbly aware of yourself in all respects.

When you get to this place, you can be a partner in a relationship with both giving and taking, loving and being loved, seeing and being seen, valuing and being valued. You will know your own worth as one half of a couple—and will no longer see yourself as being responsible for fulfilling your partner's needs.

When you find yourself attracted to powerful, important people and want to work alongside them, be careful not to identify too much with them. Maintain your own sense of self and your knowing about who you are, what your strengths and weaknesses are, and stay in tune with your feelings. In this way, you can contribute significantly to your boss's success and still feel at peace with your role and position. If you don't do this, you may find yourself becoming depressed when you realize how much you have contributed to your boss's achievements—and how little you've received in return.

By staying true to yourself, you will avoid issues with feeling restricted or as if your personal freedom has disappeared, and you won't have to alter your personality or way of being to attract a mate. You can relax and be yourself, authentically and honestly, and know that when they are drawn to you, it's truly you they are seeing. This will enable you to have relationships that have staying power.

Remember that you have a tendency to feel privileged and special, which is fine as long as you keep it in balance with your appreciation for others and their unique qualities and abilities.

> As you make these changes and learn more about yourself, you may experience a period of deep sadness and personal loss that results in depression.

Don't worry; this is a transformational period that will lead you to more accurate self-awareness and self-appreciation. If it does occur, it's just a part of your path as you evolve into your best self.

Imagine the feeling of self-knowledge and freedom as you move away from the co-dependent, needy, hidden, anxious self who had no knowledge of your own needs. And when you do, you will open yourself up to a larger version of self: the nurturing Two.

You will be well on your way to supporting and nurturing yourself and others as the tuned-in, aware, genuine, truly loving self you were meant to be!

I can't stand the inefficiency and incompetence of others.

I really can't stay for long. I have so much on my plate right now.

I love networking and meeting successful, influential people.

They did a good job, but I'm sure that I could do it

Don't disturb me when I'm working.

Type Three
The Doer

I hope I make a good impression.

I am what I do.

A productive day is a good day.

I have a deep-seated fear of rejection.

When I go on holiday, I always take my work with me.

At my best, I am giving, responsible, and I value and respect my partners. I'm also well regarded in my community.

Don't waste my time by talking trash.

At my worst in my relationships, I can be defensive, controlling, and consumed with work and projects.

3

Type Three—The Doer

As a Type Three (the Doer), you strive for success and achieve it! You enjoy excelling and are driven to create an impressive image in the world. Ideally, you want to be seen as the winner, victorious in all you undertake, and an example of a person who has it all together. You want to be admired—and receiving accolades and attention stoke your fire since you are worthy and deserving of the rewards and praise.

To say you are a goal-oriented overachiever is an understatement. Your motto might as well be, "Why just do if you can overdo!" You keep to-do lists and may even add items to the list that you've already finished, just so you can have the pleasure of crossing them off!

You like to stay busy and have little patience for people who laze about or drift aimlessly. There is a part of you that enjoys giving advice to others on how to succeed, and when they follow your suggestions, they do well.

> The taskmaster Three's greatest virtue is your industrious nature coupled with a positive attitude.

On the opposite side of the coin is your vice: vanity. You engage in a form of self-deception by sometimes confusing the image you've created of yourself with who you really are.

Constantly trying to be number one can be exhausting, and you are at risk of burning out. You have a difficult time asking for and receiving assistance because you perceive it as a sign of weakness. And you feel like you always have to be on for the world; that can be very tiring.

Because you associate who you are with what you do for a living, what you produce, or what outcomes you create, you have a difficult time being still and allowing your feelings

49

to come to the surface. While you are able to think about feelings intellectually, you rarely indulge in actually experiencing them. It just doesn't feel safe to you.

Safety is important to you. You value yourself based on your performance, and you think that everyone else does as well. At some point in your growth process, it will be important for you to really know that you are more than your work output.

> At your best, you will recognize your value as a human being and know that "doing" is just one aspect of who you are.

When this occurs, you may find yourself wanting to do more charity work or reaching out to others. In the past, you may have been too busy to find time for these more touchy-feely activities.

In a Positive, Healthy State

The need to be appreciated, admired, and seen as competent and valuable overrides all else in your life. You work tirelessly on self-promotion and accomplishing goals; as a result, others admire your efforts and performance. This admiration feeds you and helps you feel satisfied and balanced in life.

Because you are so motivated and concerned about status and how you are perceived, you have learned to quickly adapt to your environment. You can take on whatever role is needed in order to fit in and succeed. And while this can be a very helpful attribute, you are at risk of losing your sense of self if you become too chameleon-like.

As the winning Three, you speak the language of efficiency, goals, completion, and doing. You sometimes forget that you are a human being; you feel more like a human *doing*. At times, your push to get lots of things done, and done quickly, can make you almost robotic. At times like these, others' opinions of you will wane.

> The downside of this is that it's hard for you to relax because you'd rather be initiating new projects.

If you ever slack off and aren't working as hard, invariably you'll receive less admiration from your colleagues—and this feels terrible. You will strive even harder to become more task-focused and more efficient at managing your time so you can recover that position upon the pedestal. For it is there that you feel your best.

You continuously seek admiration and applause, are overly focused on your "audience," and are quick to promote and showcase your talents and accomplishments. So while you work well as part of a team, if you are not the proud peacock strutting around and showing off, you won't blend into the crowd and be just one of the team.

Remember that while everyone loves a star, when the show is over, that isn't the kind of love that endures and upon which you can build relationships. A good point of awareness for you is to recognize that when you feel super-efficient and are pushing yourself like a machine, then you have lost touch with your centre and are no longer living from your heart.

In A Detrimental, Unhealthy State

A deep-seated fear of rejection causes you to feel competitive, and at times even hostile, towards others as a way of defending yourself and your value. Unfortunately, this makes people admire you less and further escalates your feelings of fear. The cycle feeds itself and makes you miserable. But because you're not in touch with your feelings, you really don't know that you're afraid of being rejected—all you know is how badly you feel.

You tend to mistake what you do (or what you accomplish) for who you are; you become anxious when you think that your carefully manicured image might be unmasked (and your true self revealed).

You avoid failure at all costs—and in order to successfully avoid it—you have developed a belief that emotions equate to weakness. You may swallow your feelings or repress them because you see them as obstacles to your momentum and efficiency.

> Unfortunately, this creates problems when your stifled emotions come up at unexpected times and surprise you.

At times like this, you may resort to over-stressing your body through excessive exercise and working out until you're exhausted—all in your drive for accomplishment and beauty. Be careful of the tendency to try starvation diets, consume excessive amounts of coffee and other stimulants (over-the-counter, prescription, or street drugs), and to become a workaholic. You may even try to perfect your image through an abuse of cosmetic surgery or other cosmetic enhancements. None of these roads will lead you to feeling better about yourself.

The way to break this unhealthy cycle is to stop being competitive and to focus on self-improvement that is healthy and good for you. Think in terms of moderation and variety instead of focusing on one avenue or activity. Your efforts to improve yourself will gain the attention and admiration of others, and you will once again feel happy and balanced.

Tips for Getting Along with Threes

You might want to share some important points with close friends, family, or those with whom you work closely. These ideas may help others understand you better and teach them how best to interact with the energetic Three.

It's important to you that everyone leaves you alone when you're working! You are focused and on a mission; efficiency is like the Holy Grail to you.

> Interruptions are not welcome unless they will somehow make you more productive.

You respond well to open, honest feedback as long as people are not overly critical or judgmental in giving it. And you thrive on hearing how proud others are of you and your accomplishments!

As the optimistic Three, you don't want to listen to people who are talking trash, being negative, or complaining. You enjoy creating an upbeat, positive environment that is harmonious and peaceful, and you don't want to be burdened with others' problems and negativity.

On the other hand, if someone tells you how much they enjoy being around you, how inspiring you are to them, and how much they admire you and all that you've achieved, you can listen for hours!

Admirable Qualities of a Three

You are friendly, upbeat, self-assured, informed, competent, and capable. What's not to love about you? Employers fight to have you on their teams and will do almost anything to keep you; you are the productive workhorse who achieves miracles on a daily basis. Being successful and accomplishing great things has allowed you to survive and thrive in life, and most importantly, to feel loved and appreciated.

Surprisingly, you are also quite creative and are known for coming up with solutions that, while illogical to others, often work out beautifully. When you first propose your ideas, others are left speechless, not understanding what you're talking about or how it fits with the problem at hand.

You are an original and are able to shine a light on places where people are stuck, often coming up with out-of-the-box answers, to the astonishment and delight of your boss.

When your new, innovative ideas save the day, everyone is lining up to applaud you and your unique way of perceiving things!

Because of your focus on achievement, you naturally succeed in the work world and are able to provide well for your family. You are also able to recover quickly from setbacks, shake them off, and charge forward to the next challenge. This resilience is something your boss loves about you, although it's important to temper it with an understanding of your own shortcomings and areas for improvement. After all, it can't always be someone else's fault when things don't work out as you had planned!

It's important to you to stay on top of industry trends, and you pride yourself on being informed and up-to-date. And lastly, you are an excellent motivator of others—just watching you and all that you accomplish is motivation enough for most people. You make a great mentor and advisor because you enjoy supporting the desires of others to get ahead and encourage their ambitions.

Some Threes will be warm and encouraging, perhaps even seductive. Others will tend more towards being reflective, sensitive, and artistic.

A positive self-talk statement for Threes would be to say, "My feelings are as worthwhile as my accomplishments are."

Pressures and Limitations

Probably the most difficult thing for you to handle is dealing with the inefficiency and incompetence of others! You just don't tolerate laziness, ineptitude, or slackers. Threes can become overwhelmed with all that there is to do, and they may vegetate on the couch, space out and forget things, or even blow up in a temper tantrum.

In your never-ending effort to be more efficient and productive, you tend to compare yourself to those you view as successful. And you have an underlying fear of not succeeding or of others not seeing you as successful. This fear can feel constricting at times, especially when it feels like you have to hang on to the gains you've made or you might lose them.

Another challenge you face is always feeling like you're on. Since you put on a façade in order to impress others, at times you will get tired of pretending and just want to relax. But you won't allow yourself to do that for fear of losing ground in your career or seeing your fame diminish.

As Children

You may recall working hard as a child to get adults to appreciate you and notice your accomplishments. And you were probably well liked by your peers, as well as the adult authorities in your life (parents, teachers, neighbours, etc.).

You were among the most responsible of all the kids, and you could be counted on to competently complete a task or assignment. You were most likely very active in school, holding positions of leadership or diligently working in the background by serving on committees.

As Parents

Threes tend to be consistent, dependable, and loyal parents who struggle to find the balance between wanting to spend quality time playing with their children and desiring to get more work done in the office (or home office).

The good news is that you expect your children to be responsible and organized, and they grow up to have those admirable traits.

Tips for Living with Threes

In Love

As a Three, you expect to be appreciated by your partner—after all, you are the dynamic Three with the winning image and immaculate self-presentation. You enjoy being commended for your achievements; if someone compliments you on a particular quality or trait, you might not understand what they mean. When you hear praise for what you've accomplished, you understand that!

You see everything as a task to be done and improved upon, including your relationship. And you don't tolerate deep, intense feelings, negative emotions, or critical feedback. You just don't want to go there. In fact, you're likely to respond to your partner by saying, "Why don't we do something upbeat and fun?"

Be careful of this reluctance to really feel your emotions; your partner can tell the difference between you feeling things versus talking about feeling them. The performer Three may easily allow activity to replace real emotion, act the part of the perfect mate, and say the sweetest things at just the right time.

> Your loved one can help by assuring you that they love you for you— not because you're the image of a perfect partner.

One way your significant other can help you begin to experience feelings is to encourage you to slow down your activity level, especially during intimacy. This will give you a chance to feel your emotions and be affected by them.

As you halt activity (at least momentarily), your real feelings will begin to bubble up. For the controlling Three, this will be confusing, befuddling, and may produce anxiety. You may wonder if you're "doing it right" or if you're "feeling the right thing" for a given situation. The overachiever in you will try to master the act of feeling, just as you do with everything else in your life. Try to welcome the emotions. The more you can understand your own feelings, the more empathetic, compassionate, receptive, and patient you will become.

At times when your partner feels down, you may feel responsible for the negative feelings. They will need to remind you that there may not be a quick fix, and you certainly aren't in charge of making them feel better.

And because your soul and passion are for your work, your partner will need to strongly encourage and support you in taking time off. You may find it difficult to be mentally and emotionally present, even when you are physically present, during your time off. It will be helpful if you separate work and play and don't allow yourself to think about work when you are off playing.

In the Workplace

Never let it be said that the ambitious Three ever doubted his or her abilities! You perceive yourself as the instant expert about whatever you are doing. Since you think so highly of yourself in the work environment, you have a hard time delineating your work self from your real self. If you ever got fired or lost your job and didn't have a business card to hand out (telling the world how important you are), you would feel lost and unsure of who you are.

You have a habit of putting on your work like a set of clothes. You are your work.

> You live, eat, and breathe what you do for a living. You are a shining example for your profession.

Your priority is on efficiency and saving time, and sometimes you are willing to cut a few corners to achieve your goals. You may choose to multitask to save time and be sure to hit your deadline, even when it may not be appropriate or beneficial to the quality of the output. As a result of this, sometimes you overlook pesky details, thinking someone else will clean them up later.

As the taskmaster Three, you can become enraged when tasks and goals get interrupted. Your anger is specific to what isn't done right. You value the outcome over the process—and the end justifies the means. Your mantra could be to say, "How much did I produce today?"

Production is so important to you that you would rather be respected for your work ethic and output than be liked as a person. In fact, you would be hard-pressed to tell the difference between someone admiring you for your work ethos and someone actually liking you for yourself.

At times, you can be robotic in your single-minded focus to get work done, and you don't understand why others don't operate this way as well. You will continue to grow your project, larger and bigger, until someone stops you. At that point, you will look at your options and figure out the best scenario for you to come out on top and look like the winner.

One of your best characteristics is your enthusiasm and energy for your work. This rubs off on others, and they enjoy working with you when you're in your groove and thriving. Eventually you'll lose your followers since you never stop to enjoy your success. As soon as you reach one goal, you're on to the next one, crossing tasks off your to-do list with verve and passion.

Few mortals can keep up with your work stamina!

You enjoy strutting your stuff, being the proud peacock, the star performer at centre stage, and you work hard to project and maintain a finessed, high-profile image, replete with impressive credentials, social status, and being included in all the "who's who" lists. In your all-star Three mind, there is no such thing as second best.

Because of your powerhouse work ethic and the incredible results you achieve in your field, you exert power over others, and you enjoy vying for the leadership role. You like knowing what the clear path to success is in your company—and you don't deal well with ambiguity or not knowing what's required of you. You aim for specific, defined goals; in turn, you expect to be rewarded for your efforts. And it's important to you that the company have clearly defined bonus and reward programs in place—there's no room for ambiguity when it comes to your well-deserved returns!

Because of the high pedestal that you place yourself upon, you have little tolerance for failure. If things don't go the way you had anticipated on a project, you are quick to assign blame to others, switch courses of action, or find a way to spin the results so that you come out smelling like a rose. When superiors or colleagues provide you with feedback on your performance, you will have selective hearing and will only take in the positive comments.

Your worst fears in the workplace are of being nothing, of not being valuable to the company, or of appearing like you can't do what has been assigned to you. You are dynamic and industrious, and you will work hard to make sure that no matter how daunting the tasks you are asked to accomplish, they will get done—and done well.

Employers love the charming, energetic, confident, results-driven Three!

As a result you may frequently have headhunters calling on you, trying to steal you away for more money, benefits, fame, and rewards. This feeds your ego and reinforces your elevated sense of self-worth; you are happy to entertain their offers and will jump ship for a firm that goes overboard in professing your greatness.

Self-Preservation Measures

As the achiever Three, you place much emphasis on financial security. You want to have your bank account reflect your accomplishments so that you can be seen as successful in society. You will continually seek out new skills to add to your repertoire, and you always keep up with the latest industry news and trends.

> Earning your position and power is not enough—you must maintain it too.

Because you work so tirelessly, you take care to stay physically fit and in great health. You rarely take a day off of work, and when you do go on a vacation, you will likely take your work with you (much to your partner's dismay).

Success for you isn't defined as being better than others; you consider yourself successful when you best yourself, discovering how you can be better than you were last year, last month, or last week. Because you're not competitive with colleagues and you enjoy mentoring and helping others to succeed, you are a good team player. You get along well with your co-workers and avoid conflict and disagreements (partly because you just don't have time to argue—there's too much work to be done)!

In Relationships

You have perfected the art of presentation and have mastered your image. You dress to impress the opposite sex and the world at large. You rely on your charm, charisma, sexiness, strength, body image, clothing, and trappings of success to attract potential mates.

You've learned what works by paying close attention to what others find attractive, and you've modelled yourself after what society deems appealing. In addition, you are likely to alter your behaviour in whatever way is necessary to keep your partner's attention. It's important that people envy you.

You want them to be jealous of who your significant other is, how prestigious he or she is, and how special your relationship is. In fact, when you're dating, if you suspect that someone might reject you, you will avoid pursuing him or her. You just can't face failure, and you secretly believe that if they ever got to know the real you, they'd reject you for sure.

Socially

As the energetic, efficient, strong-minded Three, motivating others comes easily to you. You come up with creative solutions to problems and know how to keep people at rapt attention while you espouse your latest ideas.

Because you are a strong thinker, you focus on the overall goal of the group. With your desire to appeal to everyone, you are the one to achieve and maintain harmony within a group.

You enjoy socializing in many diverse settings, mainly because of your chameleon-like quality that allows you to adapt your personality and dress to fit into any culture.

You've found that organizations provide you with excellent opportunities to further your success. In addition, you enjoy the friendships and connections you make with other powerful, accomplished people. And because titles, degrees, credentials, and honours are so important to you, you prefer to befriend those with lots of honours and credits to their names.

For the fame-seeking Three, nothing could be worse than being anonymous. You are a natural-born performer and seek out the positive attention of others. You would be thrilled to be seen with the most famous and powerful people, and to be draped in all the trappings of success.

> Three's worldview: Since the world rewards a champion, I must avoid
> failure at all costs.

Core Issues for Threes

You've lost hope in how the universe operates. You no longer trust that things will work out naturally, and you believe that *you* must make things happen. In the past when you accomplished great things, you received praise, which felt like love to you. You realized that you could feel loved, accepted, admired, and envied if you achieved more than most people could ever dream of. In order to do this, you created a carefully crafted image of yourself.

Unfortunately, you began to believe your own lies.

Working tirelessly to achieve all that you believed would make you feel good about yourself—only to realize that your feelings of emptiness were still there—left you feeling desperate and distraught.

Sample Questions

- Am I taking short periods of time each day to slow down, feel my feelings, and reflect?
- Have I been adjusting myself to accommodate others' desires? If so, how would I like to handle that differently next time?
- When is the last time I recall actively pursuing recognition and praise (either overtly or subtly)?
- Am I focusing attention on things besides production and work?
- What other interests have I developed outside of work?
- Can I recall a recent time when I was overly worried about efficiency?
- What am I feeling? Do I like it? Can I tolerate it? What might it be signifying for me?
- The last time a feeling came up, how did I handle it? Did I welcome it?
- Are there certain feelings I feel more comfortable experiencing? Which ones?

The Core of Healing

- Stop making life a series of to–do lists!
- Release your addiction to producing and achieving more and faster.
- Learn to relax, slow down, and feel your feelings.
- Discover that love and acceptance are things you receive simply because of who you are—not as a result of what you've done.

- Give up your need to push your agenda and begin to trust that it's okay to receive in life.
- Get to know yourself, the real you, and then refuse to present any more masks to the world.
- Be authentically you.

Affirming Change

Affirmations, when used properly, are powerful tools for change. Affirmations are designed to speak directly to the subconscious mind and effect change on a level much deeper than your rational or conscious thoughts.

To use affirmations effectively, it's important to feel what you're saying and accept it as valid and real. Therefore, it's helpful to begin with an affirmation that allows you to release old beliefs and any thoughts that no longer serve you. This is followed by a positive affirmation that brings in a new idea.

Begin by saying both affirmations. Once you feel comfortable saying the second affirmation, you can drop the first one and just use the second one:

- I release my fear of being humiliated, my fear of failure, and the jealousy I feel over the success of others.
- I am more than what I do; it is safe for me to express and deal with my emotions. I can trust the love being offered to me. There is plenty for us all; the more I accept who I am, the more my true talents will shine through. I am the power in my world.

Opportunities for Growth

As a driven Three, direct some of your energies and attention towards your own evolution and growth—not just towards the projection or appearance of growth but to the actual development of yourself.

Begin by noticing when you feel fake or artificial. When you find yourself thinking, *Only I know what I'm really like—everyone else sees the mask that I project,* stop and tune into your feelings.

> Allow your emotions to bubble up to the surface for a few minutes and try to name what it is that you're feeling.

See if you can stay in that feeling state for a short time before rushing off to your next activity. At first, perhaps you will only be able to tolerate it for ten minutes. Try to build up the length of time until you can sit with your feelings, and label them by name, for thirty minutes.

If you have difficulty naming your feelings, begin with identifying how you feel physically. *My stomach is in knots. My throat feels tight and constricted.* This is a good starting point for learning about yourself and how you're feeling.

Be careful that you don't see self-improvement activities as tasks to be checked off of your to-do list. Allow yourself to really be present during these short reflective breaks in your day.

Try to identify the difference between "doing" and "feeling." Pay attention to the times when your doing becomes robotic because that is when you are avoiding feeling your emotions. Also notice when you postpone your feelings. Catch yourself saying, "I'll feel great as soon as I get that raise next month" or "We'll relax and take a family vacation after I'm vice president."

Because you have such strong talents for getting things done and done well, you think that you are always doing a great job. Notice when your fantasies of success replace your actual accomplishments. Especially watch for comments from colleagues or superiors that you've interpreted as positive that could be interpreted as areas for improvement.

Keep an eye out for unrealistic, overwhelming fears that may pop up when your work pace lessens. And when you notice things about yourself that you'd like to improve upon, stay attentive to them.

> Avoid veering off to start another project or blaming others for the last project's lacklustre results.

In your personal life, find friends and loved ones who will support you in making choices based on your feelings instead of the status or privilege you'll gain. Allow these people to love *who you are* rather than what you do or what you can do for them.

Because of your love of efficiency and production, you have a strong tendency towards being a workaholic, and you could experience manic depression (where you keep yourself manically busy so you never have to face your feelings because you believe they'd be overwhelming and you'd feel depressed). If you find yourself in this situation, seek professional help. It is something you can change. Life doesn't have to operate at a hundred miles per hour 24/7/365!

In order for the charming Three to grow and develop in a real way, you must be truthful with yourself and others. Become aware of your genuine feelings and learn to recognize your needs and how to meet them. Try to avoid bragging about yourself or inflating your importance to impress others. Your authenticity will be much more memorable and attractive than anything you could invent about yourself.

Take some time each day to connect with someone; it doesn't have to be mushy or take very long. Simply be real and genuine in your expression to them; in turn, listen to what's on the other person's mind. This will help you develop compassion and generosity in your relationships, and you will become much more loving, a true friend, and someone people really want to be around. In addition, you'll actually like yourself better!

Add "take a break every few hours" to your lengthy to-do list.

Otherwise, you'll drive yourself and others to complete exhaustion, and you will break down. There is nothing wrong with pursuing goals, but there is also no need to be relentless and motivated solely by ambition. Begin to take some time to reconnect with yourself. Take a few deep breaths, appreciate something in nature, and recharge your batteries.

Find a social project that you would enjoy contributing to and start participating. Make it something where there is absolutely no chance for you to network or achieve any career-related gain from it! You'll have a great time while learning to work cooperatively with diverse people and working towards goals that transcend your personal world. This is a powerful way to discover your inner self and your core values.

Stages of Evolution

For every personality type, there are opportunities to live from several different stages of growth, depending on whether you are reflective and interested in growing or are happy with the status quo. In addition, not everyone who is a Three will have every trait or quality described here. Some will have traces of a characteristic, and others will see that same characteristic in abundance. A general overview of each stage is followed by a more detailed description.

Deteriorating

Need admiration, self-promoting, chameleon-like, deceitful, status seeker, narcissist, unaware of needs, out of touch with feelings, arrogant, fear failure, contrived, performer, vindictive, relentless, destructive of others' happiness or success, compulsively productive/efficient, overwhelmed, burnt-out, psychopathic, suppressed rage, boiling over

As the driven Three, when you overdo it and push yourself too hard, you can reach unbearable stress levels that force you to go on autopilot. At this point, all you can think about is getting through the day. You become less interested in production and more interested in getting by, and you fall into the rut of routine and passivity.

> You may lose your focus and find yourself creating busywork just to appear competent.

If this stress cycle is not interrupted, you may start shutting down, become depressed and apathetic about life, lose interest in your work, and pull away from your loved ones. Your energy level may plummet because you have lost your enthusiasm and joie de vivre.

The truth is that you just want everyone to leave you alone. You become unyielding, stubborn, and reluctant to accept help or acknowledge that you are in trouble. At your worst, you are malevolent, vindictive, and psychopathic in your desire to derail others' success. If you aren't successful, no one else should be either!

Status Quo

Ambitious, achiever, competitive with self, passion for work/career, adaptable, very aware of self-image, seek opportunities, driven to succeed, highly concerned with others' perception of you, package yourself to meet others' expectations, premeditated behaviour, out of touch with feelings, wear mask of "having it all together," difficulty with intimacy, perceived as fake sometimes, experience instances of being caught in a lie/deceit

As the harmonious Three, you try to be diplomatic and polite. You avoid saying things that might offend others, and you strive to create balance and smooth sailing in your life. But when you feel safe in a relationship, you begin to express yourself more freely, sharing your anxieties, worries, and concerns.

You may be all smiles and positivity at work, but when you come home, you need to unload your real feelings of frustration and dissatisfaction (and it's typically your partner who bears the brunt of it).

> You feel comfortable expressing your negative feelings to your mate because you trust him or her—and you don't feel like you have to keep up any pretences.

As a result, you may spill out your doubts, suspicions, irritations at others' incompetence, and general anger. This is in stark contrast to the person your mate knew when you were dating—and certainly isn't the same person who was espousing a positive, can-do attitude at work that day!

The Alarm

As the hard-working Three, you become aware of your relentless pushing to be the victorious one, to be number one. You realize you are burning out, all in an effort to receive external validation. When you awaken, you recognize that you will only be able to live authentically and be who you are by living from your genuine self and from your true set of values. You commit to grow and become your best self.

Evolving

Practical, admired, empowering, energetic, goal-oriented, social, creative, efficient, accomplished, initiator, excel in chosen profession, good at motivating others, "together," appear impressive, beginning to recognize and identify feelings, taking time to relax, learning to separate work and play

As the resourceful Three, you realize that there is more to you than the social-climbing, pretentious, ambitious over-achiever. You begin to release your fear of failure and feelings of unworthiness.

> You start to feel less competitive with others and more likely to buoy others' careers and accomplishments.

You begin to really feel your emotions, are able to identify what you're feeling and why, and have skill sets for appropriately dealing with positive and negative emotions. You have learned to relax and have discovered that you get great satisfaction from working cooperatively with others on shared goals.

You freely give assistance, support, guidance, and advice to people in your life; even more importantly, you have opened up to receiving help when you need it! It has been a welcome surprise to you (and a great relief) to learn that others are more than willing to pitch in and help you.

You have become more patient and realistic about deadlines and workloads. As a result of this softening around the edges, you are learning to trust people and have developed some long-term connections and deep, abiding friendships.

You are more willing to put yourself out there. You are less opportunistic and more generous in looking out for others as well as yourself. You exhibit more courage and embody the qualities of a true leader. By letting go of your need to be the centre of attention and your compulsive need to produce, you are no longer a human *doing* and have become an exemplary human *being*.

On Your Spiritual Path

Accept self, reflective, authentic, genuine, in touch with feelings, charitable, humble, compassionate, empathetic, benevolent, kind, excellent mentor/advisor, generous, meet your own needs, heart-centred action, understanding

As a result of all your efforts to look at yourself and question what wasn't working, you have grown and changed tremendously! You have reclaimed your sense of honesty and restored your hopefulness in mankind and in life.

> While you are still one of the most interesting people in the room, you no longer desire to be the focus of everyone's attention.

You know your self-worth and don't need to hear compliments from others in order to feel happy and peaceful. You are filled with self-love in a calm, unassuming, modest way. You know what it means to self-sacrifice for the greater good, and you enjoy volunteering your talents to help others. People come to you for advice and guidance, and you happily share your hard-earned wisdom.

You no longer seek external acceptance or recognition because you now experience a deep connection to your inner essence, your core. You know—without a doubt—who you are, and you are enjoying your life! You are a gentle, kind, caring, extraordinary human being.

Type Three: The Doer

You are the workhorse, the achiever, and the one who always looks fabulous (in person and on paper). Others admire your drive, accomplishments, and inimitable presence.

Because it is so important to you to always look good, you may resort to fudging or distorting things a bit in order to look your best.

> Since you have a hard time accepting blame when things go wrong, you may attribute them to others or to external causes.

No matter what happens to you in life, you will not describe it as a failure; in your mind, you simply do not fail. There is always a plausible explanation for why the situation was a challenging one and how you did a great job despite the issues you had to face. Be careful because this Pollyanna attitude won't sit well with most employers. Companies are looking for someone who is balanced in his or her self-view and who can accept personal mistakes and shortcomings and work to improve upon them.

You place a great deal of emphasis on competition, but it's not against others. Instead, you compete against yourself, always striving to be better. You may enjoy working out and ensuring that you present a polished, buff body as your image to the world.

Your gifts are your abilities to solve problems, get things done, and motivate others to follow you. You see yourself as successful and finessed. The flipside of this is that you have a deep-seated fear of failure, and you might go to great lengths to avoid it (including lying, cutting corners, or misrepresenting things).

By discovering what's true about you at your core, you will recover your ability to hope, and you'll find that you can present yourself to the world as you are (not primped and buffed like a retouched image). Stop adjusting your image to suit others—and start showing them your essence. The world will love the genuine Three!

When you stop valuing yourself in terms of your performance and how you compare to society's unrealistic standards of perfection, you will begin to know your true self. It may take a significant failure or loss in your life before you will succumb to your feelings, slow down, and really question what you are all about.

> At your best, you are self-assured but not cocky, self-loving but not narcissistic, and driven but not hostile.

You are the builder of teams, the idealist who throws out the new idea and inspires an organization to change.

The popular Three is a magnet to people and can be a fantastic mentor. When you realize your full potential, you are highly social, practical, and empowering—and you have it all together. And then your *doing* can include making a difference in the world!

Type Four
The Dreamer

Something is missing. Others have it, and I feel left out and abandoned.

Don't tell me I'm too sensitive or am overreacting.

I like to be seen doing things in style.

I hope I didn't sound stupid.

I feel like I'm missing out.

The grass is always greener on the other side.

When is my real life going to begin?

I feel guilty if I disappoint people.

My looks, manners, mood, and luxury compensate for how I feel on the inside.

At my best, I'm empathetic and supportive.

At my worst in relationships, I'm self-absorbed, needy, and moody.

I'm a good friend to those in need.

I can exclude everything else that is going on around me and ignore the necessities of day-to-day survival while I pursue my goals.

4

Type Four—The Dreamer

As Type Four (the Dreamer), you are dramatic, moody, and expressive. Nothing can be mundane for you. If you feel too calm, you will typically become bored and will need to stir something up (loss, drama, or despair) so you can feel intensely again.

Your desire is to be the gifted original, the one who adheres to the highest standards, who has a unique approach to life, and who lives from intuition and insights. You long to be passionate, authentic, and connected to the vast inner world of your emotions. Your self-perception is of a spiritual, idealistic, special person who is very accomplished.

> Much of your life revolves around needing to understand yourself and needing to feel understood by others.

You seek out experiences in life that are filled with richness, depth, meaning, and emotion. Because you abhor the boredom of calm, neutral emotions, you would much rather deal with trauma, pain, angst, and other negative feelings so you can feel fully alive.

As a result of this, you are a great person to have around when a friend is in crisis or emotional turmoil. You can be with them comfortably. You aren't afraid to delve into the emotional depths where others dread to go. And you have a natural gift for being able to differentiate between the subtleties of emotions that others typically overlook.

With an artist's temperament, you want nothing more than to express yourself fully and freely and to feel accepted in that expression. Unfortunately, you are very self-conscious, almost to the point of it being painful to you. You focus much of your attention on how you are different from others, and you interpret this as a bad thing.

The good news is that when you can examine yourself and identify your unique strengths and talents, you can stop comparing yourself to others and begin to focus on what you have rather than on what you're lacking. This self-reflection will be very beneficial to you; it's vital to the introspective Four's mental health and well-being.

> Studying your inner landscape will allow you to understand yourself better, and that will bring you peace.

You tend to be quite nostalgic and like to spend time thinking about the past. Sometimes this guides you to deeper insights, and other times it is like the proverbial rabbit hole—and you disappear into a downward spiral of sadness or painful feelings. And you have a wonderful self-deprecating sense of humour that is fed by your natural lean towards navel-gazing and self-absorption.

This intense focus on you can be both a blessing and a curse. The personal awareness you receive from it is the blessing; the appearance of being egotistical and disinterested in others is the curse. When you learn how to wrangle your emotions with some clarity and understanding, you will be ready to launch yourself out into the world, to express yourself in an extraordinary way, and to be the unique original that you always knew you were!

In a Positive, Healthy State

Your compulsive need for self-understanding and clarity drives you to open up to rising unresolved, painful feelings. You are not afraid to walk through the fire of your emotions because it is that important to you to come out the other side. And this is the path that works best for the brooding Four.

Examining your feelings under a microscope, feeling every aspect of your emotions, and connecting them to other aspects of yourself (i.e. why you are the way you are) will help you fully understand yourself.

> When you feel like you know yourself, your world is right.

You are the individualistic, expressive Four! Going out into the world is only meaningful if you can carve your own distinctive swath through life. You want people to stand up and take notice of your artistic nature, your gifted expressions, and your many accomplishments. You must express your creativity in order to feel fulfilled—whether it's decorating your own space or creating a new type of art. Putting your personal signature on whatever you do is important to you!

Deeply intuitive and able to transform painful experiences into profound personal growth and huge transformative leaps, you will search out what you need in life—or you'll simply create it yourself. You look for meaning in everything, and you are keenly aware of what's missing in your life. This can lead to feelings of melancholy, nostalgia, and longing for what you don't have.

The powerful Four knows that all emotions have value and all human beings have a unique individuality. Because of this perspective on life, you are able to transform the dull and mundane into something exquisite and outstanding, fresh and novel. You breathe new life into anything you touch because you can find something to appreciate, something special or rare, in everything and everyone.

You want to surround yourself with beauty, really feel your world, and see yourself as an individual who is unlike anyone else. You value self-honesty and take full responsibility for your feelings. You are open to looking at yourself and to seeing your contradictions and shortcomings without denying or minimizing them. More than any other type, you are intensely aware of your uniqueness, your talents, and your shortcomings.

In a Detrimental, Unhealthy State

You are self-aware, sensitive and withdrawn. You will honestly express yourself emotionally, creatively, and personally, but you are also reserved, painfully self-conscious, and even moody. Your self-absorption and temperamental nature cause you to take everything way too personally—even when it wasn't about you.

You worry that others got a better deal in life and that somehow your talents and skills are being underappreciated or overlooked. You can be hypersensitive, overly dramatic, intensely emotional, snooty, bourgeois, and envious.

Whether you realize it or not, you can come across as emotionally manipulative, overly critical, and unaware of your impact on others' feelings. You may feel somewhat depressed or melancholy and see the glass as half empty. Just remember that self-pity is not attractive on you!

> You may withdraw from others due to your heightened feelings of vulnerability and a sense of being defective and different.

You may also have a sense of feeling better than others in some aspects, causing you to feel disdainful and exempt from the rules of society.

Your deepest fear is that you have no identity, nothing unique or special about you, and no personal significance. You may pull back from society in order to protect your self-image, lick your wounds, and attend to your own emotional needs.

At your worst, you tend to overindulge in sweets, alcohol, depressants, tobacco, prescription drugs, heroin, or anything that will alter your mood. You may also become lethargic and stop exercising, become overly needy of others for emotional bolstering, or turn to excessive cosmetic surgery procedures to get rid of the aspects of you that you can't bear.

And when it comes to a significant other, you have a tendency to want someone who will rescue you from having to deal with the mundane issues of daily life, someone who sees your creative genius and will support you as you go out into the world with your expressions.

> Be careful not to get involved too deeply and become clingy; this will only chase your beloved away.

Tips for Getting Along with Fours

You might want to share some important points with close friends, family, and those with whom you work closely. These ideas may help others understand you better and teach them how best to interact with the dramatic Four.

You are very sensitive, caring, and perceptive. And because you are such a good friend to others, you desire the same in return. It's important that your friends and partner are supportive of you and compliment you abundantly. Their love and admiration help you learn to love yourself and see what's valuable in you.

Another key element is that they respect you for your special contributions, insight, wisdom, emotional finesse, and intuition. And they should be careful not to tell you that you're overly sensitive or that you are overreacting to a situation since that would only upset you more.

Close friends will know how to walk the fine line you require: when you're feeling blue, you don't always want them to help you cheer up, but you might enjoy it if they could help you lighten up a little. This is not an easy thing to balance, but those who are closest to you will quickly learn the skill of bringing levity to your periods of melancholy.

Admirable Qualities of a Four

You are such a practical thinker! You enjoy figuring out the step-by-step, how-to methods of things that many others do not want to be bothered with. And once you've come to a conclusion, you are fully prepared to defend your reasoning.

As a result, others tend to trust your wisdom, value your participation and judgment, and look to you as a rock they can depend on.

> Your voice is steady, reliable, and calm when you are participating in team endeavours—even when things get chaotic.

You have a wonderful ability to find meaning in everything and to deeply feel your experiences in life. You have an abiding admiration for all that is true, noble, and beautiful. Your aesthetic nature draws you to beautiful things, whether man-made or natural.

As the intuitive Four, your sensitivity to others is finely tuned and you are able to pick up on things that others are feeling—even when they may not know what they're feeling. This makes it easy for you to develop strong, caring connections with people.

The world sees you as a unique individualist, and having others perceive you as one-of-a-kind is just as important to you as being one is! You deeply want people to notice you and understand you and your feelings.

Pressures and Limitations

The same qualities that make you so sensitive also contribute to the dark moods, melancholy, emptiness, and despair you feel. When you get in these gloomy periods, feelings of self-loathing, shame, and unworthiness take over. You can convince yourself that you just don't deserve to be loved as everyone else does.

In addition to this feeling of being undeserving, you fear abandonment by those you care about. When you disappoint them, you feel guilty about it—and you also put yourself down.

You simply expect too much of yourself and of life.

If your closest friends misunderstand you or your emotions, you may feel hurt or even attacked. These painful feelings create a longing in you for people who will truly understand your unique nature and gifts.

In general, you tend to long for what you don't have (or what you perceive you don't have). This is a lifelong dilemma for you, but it is solvable. Be careful not to obsess over resentments you've built up; this behaviour will only harm your relationships and create unnecessary pain for you.

As Children

You may recall having a very active imagination as a child, playing alone or organizing your friends in an original game that you made up. Despite your ability to lead the other children in a game, you felt like you didn't fit in with them.

Your extremely sensitive nature led you to believe that you were missing something that everyone else had.

You may have found yourself overly attached to adult authority figures you idealized (teachers, artists, etc.), yet you were probably very rebellious and anti-authority when you felt criticized or misunderstood.

You may have experienced the death of someone close to you or a divorce; these are common triggers for the loneliness and abandonment that you still feel as an adult.

As Parents

Fours tend to support their children's imagination, originality, and creativity, and they are very good at helping kids know, identify, and handle feelings. You do a great job of helping your children become who they really are inside, although you can sometimes be overly harsh, critical, or protective of them.

Generally though, as the emotionally deep Four, you do a good job with your kids—as long as you don't get too self-absorbed and caught up in your own internal drama.

Tips for Living with Fours

In Love

Your partner will want to always keep in mind your need for intense emotion. You get bored with the ho-hum nature and harmony of being a couple and will want to intensify things. Unfortunately, you may resort to sabotage, dramatic behaviour, or periods of deep suffering in an attempt to feel more deeply.

You look to other couples and worry that they have something that you are missing in your relationship. The thought that there must be more to it than this may cross your mind frequently.

> Relating to you is never going to be simple because you prefer a relationship with depth and meat to it to one that is easy and fun.

The distant, unavailable images of love draw you like a moth to a flame and seem much more romantic and intriguing than whatever you currently have. Your partner may be dismayed by your wistful attraction to a distant friend, a long-lost love, or an unrealized dream.

For you, living in the present moment feels limited and flat. You seek an experience of love that ultimately takes you to an awakening of your deepest self, your soul—a transformative epiphany forged by love.

For the many-layered Four, pursuing happiness is not a goal. You have a bittersweet, melancholic, emotional nature, and you have a hard time letting go of any intense feelings—even if they're painful or harmful. You may reminisce about past friends and lovers—or dream of future loves—rather than focusing your attention on the partner you currently have in your life.

For the artistic Four, life is a performance. You are careful to present yourself perfectly: the ideal attitude, the best manners, and the ultimate expressions of good taste. This wows your date and sets the stage for impressing him or her—without revealing much about your true self.

You have mastered the art of keeping yourself and your true feelings contained. You banter, create small talk, discuss the news of the day, enjoy lively talks about art and beauty, imply things with a certain glance, and generally create a mood of ideal romantic intrigue. But by the end of the night, while your date may have had a fabulous time and be fascinated with you, they really have no idea of who you are or anything concrete about you.

When your love interest responds to you with romantic gestures, you quickly pull back. When you are with them, you notice all their negative qualities. It is only when they leave for a time that you remember all the things you like about them. The safety of distance helps you see more clearly. Unfortunately, this push/pull behaviour only reinforces your deep-seated feelings of loss and abandonment.

> Your search for the special, ultimate love to complete you will not get you what you want.

Try to appreciate the qualities that you have in your relationship and let go of dreamy thoughts about what might be or what's missing. In this way, you can become content with a real, meaningful relationship in the here and now.

In the Workplace

As a distinctive Four, you seek out work that will tap your creative skills and your particular genius while providing ample berth to express yourself in business. When colleagues and superiors respect your vision and ideas, you feel at your best, valued, and seen.

Your work efficiency is directly connected to your state of mind and your mood. When your emotions are volatile, your work suffers. And a downturn in a love affair can cause you to sabotage your work life.

The artistic Four feels demeaned by drone work (how you define this will be different for each Four). You feel drawn to work that taps into your incredible strength as an emotionally deep human being; you may work as an activist, an addiction or grief counsellor, or a volunteer on suicide or abuse hotlines.

You enjoy working alone and will not do well in a team setting that requires you to collaborate with others who are more skilled or better paid. You can become aggressive and cutthroat towards those you view as competition.

On the other hand, you are attracted to people who are successful in other fields, and you desire connections with those whose work/careers represent quality and high standards.

Self-Preservation Measures

As the romantic Four, you must express yourself out in the world and want nothing more than to be seen as an original! You long for feelings of intensity and seek out stimulating experiences just to feel alive.

> Nothing is worse than living a dull, flat, monotone life; you view this as a meaningless existence.

Being near transformational periods (birth, death, catastrophic situations, and life-ending illness) feels like living to you. This is where you are in your element, where you are better able than any other personality type to be there for people and to help them bear the emotional burden of a difficult time in life.

Sometimes you'll take physical risks to stimulate your life. You may break a law, invest in a risky stock pick, become promiscuous, or get involved with someone who is clearly not good for you. Your perseverance and determination get you through these crises.

If someone attacks your lofty ideals, you feel defensive and strongly rebellious. You want no part of others telling you what to do, what to change about yourself, or what you should believe! Anyone who attempts to do so may experience your cutting sarcasm, quick temper, or belligerent rage.

When you are working for a cause you believe in, you have great intensity and focus. At times, you may forget about everything else in your life, ignoring your day-to-day necessities until you meet your goal.

> You have a creative mind and a talent for pointing out new ways of looking at things or bringing up perspectives that others have failed to consider.

Be patient when explaining these concepts to others since they are not as quick to see situations from as many angles as you are.

Finally, as a self-defence mechanism, you are known to take serious offense when people assume they know who you are, what you are thinking, or how you are feeling because you honestly believe that no one can understand you.

In Relationships

It's no surprise that you want your loved one to think that your relationship is unique, romantic, and intense. You secretly dream of a soul mate who will come along and rescue you from your boring, mundane, ordinary life.

It's difficult for you to get close in any relationship. You worry that your partner may figure out that you really aren't as good as advertised and leave you. Your deepest fear is that you're not worthy enough or special enough to deserve to be loved.

In order to avoid being dumped, you frequently create scenes that force your mate to leave you. Within days though, you'll be trying to win them back. This push–pull drama helps create the distance you want in a relationship, the chaos and intensity that you crave, and the feeling that you are in control.

> In fact, you are more interested in your partner when they are distant from you, simply due to your tendency to be drawn to that which is unattainable.

When you have disagreements or arguments with your partner, you are unlikely to get angry. Instead, you will become depressed, sullen, withdrawn, and remote.

Friendships can be challenging for you because you compare yourself with others, and you always find yourself lacking something. Everyone else seems to have something that you don't have. You find yourself envying others who appear to be happier, more fulfilled, or who seem to lead much more interesting lives.

Socially

As the overly sensitive Four, you die a thousand deaths when you make a mistake or put your foot in your mouth. You often feel inadequate at social gatherings and will either try to out-charm everyone or dissolve into the woodwork. Despite this painful feeling about socializing, you may feel slighted or shamed if you are not invited to an event that your friends are attending.

You tend to overanalyse yourself and feel ashamed that you don't measure up to your ideals and visions. You assess yourself as not smart enough, not creative enough, not a good enough activist, not a powerful enough humanitarian, not a romantic enough partner, and on and on. You may query yourself relentlessly. *Was I clear in what I said? Did I sound uneducated or ignorant? Did I go overboard and act too aggressively? Did I give in too easily?*

You feel more confident if you can take on a specific role in a group setting, ideally a role that positions you as the authority or as the trendsetter of the group. And when you're part of a group, you may say pejorative things about yourself in an effort to prevent others from feeling envious of you.

You secretly dream of achieving monumental status and recognition because this would make you feel better than those who may have put you down or belittled you in the past.

> Four's worldview: I have been abandoned. I'm missing something that others have. I am different.

Core Issues for Fours

You've lost sight of your natural state of connection to everyone and everything. Paradoxically, you believe that you've been abandoned by the world and that you are missing a key element that others have. So you spend your life seeking that perfect love or ideal experience that will make you finally feel whole, loved, accepted, and complete. You live from a place of envy and yearning for what you dream of but think is not accessible to you. Your focus is like a magnet to what is not present and what's missing.

In the ultimate irony, your continual external quest for what you're missing (when in reality, nothing is actually missing) only perpetuates your lifelong dilemma. Although your intentions are honourable and good, you are seeking something you won't find outside of you. And this unfulfilled search leaves you feeling deficient and with even more intense longings.

If you can simply switch perspectives and realize that everything you need is within you, you can experience the completeness and fulfilment that you desire. If you learn to accept and appreciate what you have—here, now, in this moment—you can know peace and happiness.

> Your change work begins from the inside out—not the other way around, dear Four.

Come to the valid conclusion that pitfalls and disappointments are just a part of life, not something singled out to pick on you or life's way of indicating your shortcomings!

Sample Questions

- How much of my life's energy and focus have been spent on looking for what's missing?
- How do I experience envy and yearning? Greater connection?
- What does it feel like when I'm disappointed with myself?
- What have my feelings been lately? Can I identify the range and intensity, the appropriateness or inappropriateness?
- In what ways have my actions been influenced or affected by my feelings?
- Am I able to stay on course even when I'm feeling melancholy or depressed?
- How have I nullified or belittled the mundane and ordinary aspects of life, including people I see as such?
- Have I felt pride in being unique and special or shame from being different?
- Have I taken things personally that really had little or nothing to do with me?

The Core of Healing

- Recognize that you are complete as you are right now; there is no finding wholeness since it is already present in you.
- Learn to appreciate yourself and the qualities, skills, and traits you already possess (focus on the glass being half full).

- Don't allow your intense feelings to dominate your life and sabotage other areas (such as work or personal). Strive for a stable course, in spite of any waves of feelings that come along.
- Begin to see the beauty in the ordinary and mundane—you are such an appreciator of beauty that this will be easy when you put your mind to it.
- Realize that feeling a need to be special and extraordinary is rising from your ego. At your core level, you can see the uniqueness in each person you meet.

Affirming Change

Affirmations, when used properly, are powerful tools for change. Affirmations are designed to speak directly to the subconscious mind and effect change on a level much deeper than your rational or conscious thoughts.

To use affirmations effectively, it's important to feel what you're saying and accept it as valid and real. Therefore, it's helpful to begin with an affirmation that allows you to release old beliefs and any thoughts that are no longer serving you. This is followed by a positive affirmation that brings in a new idea.

Begin by saying both affirmations. Once you feel comfortable saying the second affirmation, you can drop the first one and just use the second one:

- I release my feelings of hopelessness and despair and all self-sabotaging thoughts and actions. I release the need to self-indulge in my emotions and all behaviour that no longer serves me. I am not my feelings—only those feelings I act on express who I am.
- I now choose to make more empowered choices. I see and focus on the blessings in my life and allow my life to transform to something higher.

Opportunities for Growth

As the romantic Four, you feel everything intensely, deeply, and fully. When you experience a loss in your life, be sure to take time to mourn it before moving on. And when you have periods of melancholy or sadness, interrupt them with exercise breaks or by taking time to be of service to others—these will help you snap out of it.

Commit to yourself to finish what you start. Stop allowing yourself to sabotage your efforts by leaving things incomplete. And when it comes to relationships, subdue your need to act out and create drama. Teach your partner about your mood swings and how he or she can help bring levity to you when you're down. You can choose to view your mate's consistent presence as proof that he or she loves you, and this can soften your anxiety about being abandoned.

Shift your focus to what is right with your relationship and your loved one.

Recognize that intimacy will most likely trigger your deepest fears of abandonment and loss. Challenge yourself to move past the old pattern of push–pull in your relationships; the more you can appreciate what you have, the easier this will be to surmount.

When you see a quality or trait that you envy in someone else, go within and find something similar in you. For example, if you admire how a friend seems to be confident in social situations, look at yourself and find an aspect of your life where you feel confident. Perhaps you feel most assured when you are creating or designing something. Admire and appreciate the confidence you see in yourself (instead of envying it in another). You'll be surprised at the shift that will occur as a result!

Keep changing the channel from what's wrong to what's right. Make yourself look for the good in what you have in your life already. Develop a habit of gratitude.

And along those lines, recognize and become sincerely appreciative of your friends. Because of them, you can build a strong support system that will help you weather your occasional periods of melancholy and depression. At some point, you may even begin to feel the sweetness of sadness and how your comfort with it allows you to help others when they are suffering.

Because you have tried to figure out your world by interpreting your feelings—and because your feelings are volatile and shifting—you have felt tossed like a ship on the sea. When you begin to pay less attention to your emotions, recognizing that they are not a source of guidance or direction for you, you can begin to feel stable and permanent in who you are.

You are not your feelings.

Your sense of who you are cannot be tied to how you feel in any given moment because you are much more than any emotion.

Learn to read your emotions because they are telling you things about yourself (how you feel right now, if your boundaries are being crossed, if you are experiencing a loss, etc.). Emotions indicate a temporary state, not your essence.

Do things even when you're not in the mood; otherwise, you tend to procrastinate and leave much unfinished. Commit to being productive and doing meaningful work to contribute to others. In this way, you will discover who you are and your place in society and life. By expressing your talents and helping others, you will find your happiness. Staying home and hiding out is not going to help you find yourself!

As the reflective Four, you have a tendency to want to think more about things instead of jumping in and taking action. Go against your natural inclination and start putting yourself out there into the action of life! You may never feel fully ready, but so what? Go do it anyway! Start small and commit to something that will bring out your best qualities.

Start taking care of *you*, including getting enough sleep, exercising regularly, eating a healthy diet, refraining from mind-altering substances, and avoiding addictive products. Every little step you take adds up to big shifts in how you will feel physically and mentally. If you continue to indulge in excesses (sex, drugs, alcohol, sleep, fantasies), you are truly harming yourself and crippling your chances for a healthy, happy life.

In the past, you've spent hours having long, drawn-out conversations in your head, practicing what you want to say, even though you probably never actually said anything in the end. Stop this. This is playing in illusion and keeps you from being fully present in reality.

> Rein yourself back in and encourage yourself to stay grounded,
> right here, in the present.

If you want to tell someone something, just say it *aloud* to that person in real time. Live your life instead of repeating dress rehearsals in your mind.

Although the pain of your past was real, revisiting it continually in your imagination is not helping you create a life today. In fact, it does the opposite—it takes your focus to the past.

> When you intensify your feelings, it pulls you away from your authentic self and truest expression. Instead, minimize your feelings and live your life regardless of what you feel.

Making these changes, even if done little by little over a period of time, will help you reclaim your wholeness and live in the present moment. You will come to appreciate what you have (qualities in you, experiences you have, and people in your life), and you'll find a place of acceptance of self, as you are, without needing any fancy trappings or extraordinary characteristics.

Stages of Evolution

For every personality type, there are opportunities to live from several different stages of growth, depending on whether you are reflective and interested in growing or are happy with the status quo. In addition, not everyone who is a Four will have every trait or quality described here. Some will have traces of a characteristic, and others will see that same characteristic in abundance. A general overview of each stage is followed by a more detailed description.

Deteriorating

Melancholic, despairing, depressed, tormented, withdrawn, alienated, hopeless, afraid of success, filled with self-pity, angry with self, resentful, envious, loathing of the ordinary and mundane, bourgeois, snooty, disdainful, stressed, manipulative, dependent, push-pull with relationships, possessive, controlling, lost, abandoned, addicted, suffering manic-depression, shameful, reckless, disoriented, inadequate, flawed, vulgar, inauthentic, create fantasy self

As the deprived Four, you feel as if you missed out on something—like life forgot about you and remembered everyone else! You tend towards despair, hopelessness, and self-destructive behaviours. Unfortunately, you may escape through alcohol, drugs, psychological breakdowns, or suicide.

You are tormented by illusions of who and what others are or have (seeing them as better than they really are), and feeling a sense of lack in yourself and your life.

> You may feel intense self-contempt, continually criticize yourself,
> or have morbid thoughts.

Life is one huge torment to you. You find it easy to attribute all of this to being someone else's fault (certainly not your own), and this effectively creates a chasm between you and anyone you care about.

When you fail to achieve your lofty dreams, you begin to withdraw, become angry with yourself, alienate yourself from others and from life, and may even become emotionally paralysed. You feel great shame and can easily become non-functioning, a hermit in your own life.

Status Quo

Special, intensely feeling, dreamer, moody, romantic, idealist, consider yourself unique, special and extraordinary, self-absorbed, deep, always lacking something, defective, practical, methodical, rigid, not in touch with true self, fantastical thinking, dwelling on things, over-indulgent, lethargic, teller of sad stories, overly-sensitive, defensive, competitive, feeling misunderstood, controlling, critical of self and others, demanding, exacting, dissatisfied

Somehow you reached the conclusion that you are different (meaning better) than others and are exempt from the rules of living that everyone else follows! As the melancholy Four, your tendency is to become a dreamer, to feel indulgent, and to live in a fantasy world filled with decadence, sensuality, and excesses. Your envious nature and self-pity contribute to your increasingly unproductive, impractical, bourgeois view of life.

Despite the fact that your feelings continually get you into trouble in life, you continue to delve into them, considering them to be factual and self-defining.

> You like to personalize everything that occurs in the world, taking it to heart,
> even when it has nothing to do with you!

This self-absorption can lead to periods of withdrawal where you pull back from life, retreat into yourself, become depressed, feel alienated and abandoned by everyone, and allow your moods and deep emotions to overshadow your daily life.

To you, it feels like these retreats are a way to protect yourself, to delve into your deeper nature, and to sort things out; in reality, they take you deeper down the rabbit hole and will never lift you up to the light.

The Alarm

When you become aware of your pattern of gripping and intensifying your feelings through the use of your mind and your imagination, you can come to the realization that this is not working for you! And because you understand that to get a different outcome, you have to do something differently, a light goes on in your head. Your eureka moment is a turning point in your life. Now you can begin to connect to your inner self in a new way—by ignoring your feelings and going directly to your essence (your inner knowing). Living from there enables you to begin to connect with reality, appreciate yourself, and start to express your creativity.

Evolving

Inspired, intuitive, sensitive, expressive, revealing, aware of self, recognizes and appreciates beauty in all things, creative, refined, finessed, artistic, unique, imaginative, romantic, idealist, understand self, emotionally healthy, balanced, satisfied, self-disciplined, realistic, live in the real world, present in the moment, enjoy life, extend self into community, generous volunteer, interested in helping others, supportive, understanding, empathetic, engaged

As the artistic Four, you see life through the eyes of the romantic, beautiful, and sublime! You enjoy creating an aesthetic environment and want to infuse your life with passion and imagination.

You are a true individualist, stay true to yourself, and are honest with your feelings.

A humanitarian by nature, you enjoy helping others and being emotionally available for them during their darkest hours. You are able to be serious and whimsical, gentle and strong. You are self-aware and thoughtful. Your search for self has led you to a wonderful place where you are aware of your feelings and can keep them in the proper perspective.

You don't feel a need to respond to every impulse or emotion anymore, and you know how to ignore feelings that are not helpful in the moment. You have developed your compassionate side and are highly sensitive and intuitive. Others love to be around you because you always know what they're feeling—and what to say or do to make them feel even better!

On Your Spiritual Path

Connected to source, living with meaning, balanced emotionally, equanimous, temperate, happy, peaceful, appreciative, grateful, courageous, open, expressive, original, profoundly creative, contributor to society, honest, sincere, authentic, loving, gifted, talented, curious, strong, powerful, self-confident, humble, socially at ease, have a clear sense of self and identity, connected to others, feel understood and seen, accepting of mood changes, able to express the personal and the universal, self-renewing, transformative, sensitive, funny, vulnerable, compassionate, gentle, tactful

You have found that you have within you all that you could ever want or need—and it's magnificent! You have arrived at a place of bliss and peace, content with yourself and life.

> You are now able to tap into your boundless font of creativity and can express yourself in an original way.

When you create, you do so from the personal and from the universal—representing our collective feelings and experiences through your creations. This is why others feel so moved and touched by your work.

You are able to renew and regenerate yourself and transform your life experiences into meaningful, profound understandings that affect you and those you share them with. Contributing to society and helping others has become your touchstone, and you can't live without opportunities that benefit others on a daily basis.

Beauty is everywhere in your life, and you see it in everything from the most mundane fire hydrant to the most exquisite flower. You feel compelled to share this beauty with others, especially the inner beauty that you see inside each person. As a result, people are very drawn to you and actively vie to be in your company.

Type Four: The Dreamer

You are the passionate, empathetic, intense, artistic Four! You're an individualist who wants to be seen as unique, one-of-a-kind, and extraordinarily special. Perhaps you are an artist, but no matter what, you find a way to express yourself creatively.

You feel life deeply and grow bored with too much of the ordinary. For you, the everyday can be tedious. Diving into the depths of your feelings, sitting with others who are in crisis, or being embroiled in a relationship drama make life exciting and palpable to you.

> You're on a quest to understand yourself, to explore the secret of life's meaning, and to master your emotional landscape.

It is common for you to bring out the beauty in everything in your world—from how you decorate your home to the clothes you wear.

Unfortunately, you don't see the beauty in yourself because you are too busy worrying about what others have that you don't have, feeling like you've missed out on something important in life, and wondering if you've been left behind.

Underlying this artistic, sensitive nature of yours is a deep fear of not being unique, not being special enough, and of being abandoned as a result. This evidences itself in your periodic episodes of melancholy, sadness, and depression. At these times, you withdraw from society and try to understand yourself better.

When you realize that your feelings are not the equivalent of you (they are not who you are), you can begin to discover your authentic self. By learning to experience the present moment fully and to appreciate the richness and beauty of what you have and who you are, you can heal your wounds and blossom into your fullness.

By connecting to your inner self, your highest nature, you can unearth true meaning. When you are able to balance your emotional side with acceptance and tolerance—and learn to keep those volatile feelings under control—you feel content and happy.

For as the sensuous Four, you have the innate ability to enjoy and relish every aspect of life's beauty—if you only have the courage to get past your fears and creatively share your natural talents with the world. When you do this, you will touch the lives of many in profound ways!

Type Five
The Agent

The more time I spend with people, the less energy I have. I need my space.

Don't pressure me or make me feel obligated.

Great! They're all chatting amongst themselves; I can sit here quietly and observe.

Don't expect me to reply. I need time alone to process my feelings and thoughts.

I can easily create order from chaos, but I detach and withdraw when I am stressed.

I wish I could get out of the meeting.

At my best, I'm kind, perceptive, trustworthy, and open-minded.

I love time out to think quietly by myself.

At my worst in a relationship, I can be suspicious, withdrawn, and negative.

I'll tell her exactly what I think … when I get around to it.

Privacy is a key issue in my life. I'm often detached and curious, and I like others to see me as perceptive, logical, and knowledgeable.

5

Type Five—The Agent

As Type Five (the Agent), you are cerebral, informed, original, and secretive. You find the world feels intrusive to you, and you seek out time to think quietly by yourself. You enjoy seeing yourself as an intellectual, detached, and curious. You would like others to see you as perceptive, logical, thoughtful, and knowledgeable.

Privacy is a key issue in your life, and you loathe social gatherings where there will be many people and lots of frivolity because it feels like chaos. You tend to cling to the sidelines when out in public and are not forthcoming or social; you rue having to reveal yourself to others.

Preferring to be a detached observer, the world feels overwhelming and demanding to you. As a result, you prefer to isolate yourself in order to achieve a quiet, calm place where you can think and access your feelings.

> Energetically, the world requires too much of you and seems to give you very little in return.

You pride yourself on being wise and scholarly, and you will develop a deep level of expertise in areas that interest you, sometimes in more than one field. You may have several graduate or postgraduate degrees to your name because you believe knowledge equates to power and is a prerequisite for survival.

You may be a scientist or in another studious profession where your unmatched abilities to perceive and observe win you praise and respect. As the detached Five, you are able to stand back and watch the world, unaffected by your feelings. Your investigative nature and unquenchable appetite for new information have you reading continually in your fields of interest.

But you don't just spout back what you know. You take time to develop insights about how things work, how people or systems work, and how the world works—and only then will you share your conclusions with others.

You enjoy knowing things that others don't know, and sometimes you use information as a weapon to accumulate power or position. You take secret pleasure in withholding information when you know someone really wants it! Your baser nature may even have you involved in blackmail or behaving in a superior, condescending manner towards others.

> Your general approach to life is to observe and analyse in an effort to understand the world.

You feel balanced and healthy when you comprehend how the world works. And when you lose touch with that understanding, you feel overwhelmed by life, people, and events. You may become defensive, withdrawn, or isolated.

In a Positive, Healthy State

As the dispassionate Five, your self-perception is of someone who is introspective, innovative, intelligent, and self-sufficient. You enjoy being intense and different from others. You are the one who is willing to point out that the emperor has no clothes, and you have a unique sense of humour that points out the absurdities in life.

Your clear objectivity, insight unaffected by emotion, and natural instinct are some of your greatest strengths. You know how to pull together disparate pieces of information and create order from chaos. You love to create systems that will help you organize, categorize, and analyse data more efficiently and clearly.

Your keen mind enables you to notice, assess, and monitor every aspect of a project, including the tiniest details. Employers love having you around because of your systematic thinking and objective assessments!

> You are also great in an emergency, remaining calm and detached from all the drama.

Much of your focus in life is spent on observing the external world, hiding yourself from others, collecting information (because to you, information is power), and protecting yourself from the craziness of the world. You are not one to rely on intuition—cold, hard facts are what you seek in your quest for reason and logic.

You enjoy systems, patterns, having the correct tools for the job, being informed, approaching things rationally, and meeting the world in the realm of the mind where you feel most comfortable.

As the adaptable Five, you have a very flexible, quick mind. You are great with coming up with on-the-spot solutions and can talk yourself into or out of a tight spot easily. You worry less about being right and more about winning at any cost. Your inventive mind drives you to reinvent things in a new way, with a new approach, and helps you turn around bad situations so that they come out in your favour.

You have created a mental map of the world and how you believe it works, and this is important to you. Without this map, you would feel lost and overwhelmed by it all. But it's important to remember that a mental construct is not the same as actual experience!

Despite your retiring shyness and controlled presence, deep inside, you have a gentle heart and are supportive and loyal to friends you know you can trust.

In a Detrimental, Unhealthy State

When you are unable to process how the world works or how people operate, you can easily become overwhelmed by life. Your solution is to detach and withdraw into isolation where your feelings are clear to you—even though you don't have the words to express them to anyone else.

> You enjoy obtaining a feeling of power in life—a power that comes from not needing anything.

You think you don't need people, a social life, connections, or anything else besides knowledge. You understand information easily, and it can be used to achieve your goals.

You tend to avoid the scrutiny of others, and if you feel inferior, you are likely to disappear into the woodwork and vanish from sight. However intelligent you may be, there are times when you feel that you lack intellect, and this causes you to feel vulnerable and on display.

Much like a cowering animal, you retreat to your den to lick your wounds and recharge your batteries. Being in the world takes a lot from you. It drains you, and as a result, you require a lot more alone time than most people do. It is essential that others not demand too much of you or drain your time or energy—and that your life stays simple and unfettered. You need to be in control of your environment, time, and energy.

You do not want to participate in small talk or groupthink sessions since you consider them a total waste of your time. And you'll avoid drawing attention to yourself in a meeting for fear of being misunderstood or perceived as uneducated.

> While you see yourself as original and thoughtful, others may perceive you as antisocial, distant, reclusive, cold, or eccentric.

Your Achilles' heel is avarice—greediness with yourself, your emotions, your thoughts, your energy, your time, and even your things. This can create a chasm between you and the people in your immediate world. You have a tendency to peer out at life from a safe hiding space, which causes you to be out of touch with others' feelings and concerns. Indeed, sometimes co-workers and associates describe you as arrogant, reserved, or unfeeling.

Your deepest fear is of being annihilated and destroyed by life. You are averse to being fully present in your body and with your emotions because that is a scary way to live. You are much more comfortable living in your mind. Since you prefer a simple, uncluttered lifestyle, free of too many attachments (to people or things), you will not stockpile things. All you require is access to information through books, newspapers, magazines, the library, or the Internet.

At your worst, you may resort to minimizing your own needs. This could result in bad hygiene habits, poor nutrition, inconsistent sleep habits, little to no exercise, or even turning to psychotropic drugs or narcotics for stimulation or relaxation.

Tips for Getting Along with Fives

You might want to share some important points with close friends, family, and those with whom you work closely. These ideas may help others understand you better and teach them how best to interact with the analytical Five.

You enjoy your alone time and are not forthcoming emotionally—even with your significant other. As such, you need a partner who is very independent and does not invade your personal space or require too much of you. To get your attention, he or she should speak in a direct, concise manner since you don't have time to listen to the long version of the story!

Your mate will want to leave you alone so that you can process your thoughts and feelings, and he or she will need to realize that if you appear distant or aloof, it's most likely because you are feeling uncomfortable. You want to feel welcome and appreciated, but if your mate overdoes it, you will question his or her honesty and sincerity.

It takes you a while to distil things in your mind and come to a conclusion—and then it takes even more time and effort to find the words to express yourself aloud. If your partner makes you repeat yourself, you may become irritated or frustrated.

> You need a loved one who is genteel and doesn't bulldoze you with his or her energy and physical presence.

Your loved one will also need to be okay with avoiding large parties, loud settings, excess emotions, and any invasion of your privacy because these are the things you require in order to feel comfortable.

Admirable Qualities of a Five

As the investigative observer Five, you have a detached and objective view of life. You enjoy standing back and seeing things from an arm's length. In your mind, there is no sense in getting bogged down in the emotion and drama of the situation when you can easily take notes from the sidelines! You enjoy reaching a deep and thorough understanding about your world and the people in it.

> You notice causes and effects, systems and processes, what works, and what doesn't work.

You are great in a crisis because you remain calm and keep your wits about you. Integrity is a keystone of your personality; you must do what you perceive to be right, and you take pride in not being influenced by outside pressures.

You have a disdain for acquiring material possessions or achieving status of any kind. Interestingly enough, you can never acquire enough knowledge or information! Your basic tenet is that there is always something else to be gleaned, known, or garnered from any line of inquiry. Be careful that you are able to discern when enough is enough; sometimes gathering more data simply confuses the issue and delays decisions.

You are strong willed and know when it's appropriate to give in and when to stand your ground—and when to contribute information and when to withhold it in order to achieve the greatest impact. Your perceptive nature allows you to collect data so that you can better understand your environment, and you excel at this assessment process!

Pressures and Limitations

As the observer Five, it can be frustrating to watch others (who are better social navigators) do better than you professionally, especially because they are not as skilled technically or as intelligent as you are!

But although you have a greater understanding of the concepts, processes, systems, and a broader knowledge base on the subject, you are too slow to contribute your insights, and others tend to beat you to the punch.

> Because knowledge is so valuable to you and equates to power in your mind,
> you can come across as a know-it-all.

This can feel frustrating to you when you reflect on the situation. You also regret times when you act defensively (like when others question your conclusions, and you know they're correct!).

You really don't like idle chitchat at social gatherings, and you only attend these events when you feel pressured to do so. And although you agree to be present, you regret spending time with people you don't want to be with.

As Children

You may recall spending a lot of alone time as a child, reading, collecting special things, or playing by yourself. You probably had a select group of friends who were important to you. You were an intelligent, curious student and did well in school. Your teachers enjoyed having you in class, and you were quick to learn new subjects.

Your independent style of thinking had you questioning authority figures frequently, especially your parents and teachers. At times, you may have felt as if the adults were intruding on you and trying to manage you too closely, or you may have felt like they were not paying enough attention to you and neglecting you.

You had a tendency to stand back and watch life from a distance with a detached perspective. You enjoyed taking mental notes and collecting data about life. You kept a neutral expression so that others never saw you appear afraid or worried.

> You were a sensitive child and tried your hardest to avoid any kind of confrontation or conflict.

As Parents

Fives tend to be very sweet, loving parents who are tuned into their child's life experiences. Your devoted nature may sometimes come across in more authoritarian ways, and you may order your children around a bit.

In addition, because you are so intellectually gifted, you expect a great deal from your children in this arena, perhaps having expectations that are beyond what your children are capable of developmentally. Be careful about this.

Because you are not easily in touch with your emotions, it can be challenging for you to deal with your children's emotions, especially because children have such intense feelings and express them with abandon. Be cautious that you are tolerant of your children's emotions and that you don't shut them down—you wouldn't want to teach them your habits in this arena.

Tips for Living with Fives

In Love

It takes time to process your emotions; most likely, you are not able to respond at the time a situation is occurring. Instead, you'll need time to sort through your feelings and reflect on what happened. This results in delayed reactions—and most likely will require getting back to your partner with your thought-out response.

You enjoy time alone since it feels intimate to you; it refreshes you and is as necessary as breathing is. Your loved one will need to tolerate these periods of time apart from you.

> You have an interesting ability to develop strong connections with people and very sweet feelings for them—without the need for a lot of talking or interaction.

Some people will get this aspect of you and will be okay with it, but others will interpret it as you being disconnected and uncaring.

Unfortunately, when you feel intimately connected to someone, it can trigger a need for you to detach. The underlying message you send to your partner is "I can live without you" or "I love you but don't need you."

You have a tendency to compartmentalize your relationship, and your significant other may only be invited into certain aspects of your life. Obviously, this does not go over well with your mate and can cause disastrous consequences for the relationship.

You have a need to withdraw and do this in a cyclical pattern. You appreciate having your partner draw you out of your shell and re-engage you in the relationship because you can get caught between desiring connection and wanting to be left alone.

Your beloved will need to understand that your language of love is based upon action. In other words, you will express your love in nonverbal ways, such as washing the car, doing the dishes, or leaving a treat on the pillow. You are more in touch with your feelings when you are physically expressing them than if you are forced to verbalize them. Sexual intimacy is a great connector for you.

When you feel emotionally attached to your mate, you may become possessive and feel as if your partner is your emotional life preserver, keeping you afloat. Despite this dependency on your loved one, your typical way of handling emotions is to not get too involved—even though it's your life we're talking about preserving!

Your significant other will need to learn to read and interpret your signals properly or there will be a lot of miscommunication and hurt feelings. When your beloved notices you are feeling jealous or angry, the good news is that you are feeling *something*—and that means you are more connected than usual. When you aren't feeling anything, it's a sign that you are much more detached and uninvolved in the relationship.

> You can be very supportive of your mate when you are not feeling pressured or obligated to do anything or to respond to his or her needs.

Unfortunately, very few partners who are willing to wait around until you feel inspired to support them; they typically have needs and want them to be met in a timely manner!

In the Workplace

Since you do not have an endless supply of energy, it's important to parcel out your time and energy wisely, which means you won't want to contribute it towards others' agendas!

As the self-reliant Five, you will work diligently in order to get some freedom and privacy in your life. In other words, you work hard to earn your independence.

You require routine and the ability to predict what's next so that you can be fully prepared for things when they arise. You are the one who notices if the last meeting's minutes were not distributed or if the agenda and attendees are not listed for the next meeting!

> You work best on your own since others can prove to be very distracting to you.

It can feel as if others are intruding upon you, and you may find it hard to focus when others are around. Because you feel the need to be prepared, you don't respond well to impromptu questions about your work. You might stutter or freeze, and you need time to isolate and reflect on matters before you feel comfortable giving an answer.

Conflict is a four-letter word to you, and you will avoid it at all costs! As a non-threatening Five, you will create a barrier of assistants, e-mails, and messages to keep you safe from any dramatic office scenes.

You place a high value on making decisions objectively and without emotion. When you observe others making choices based on emotion, you perceive them as out of control. As a result, you can be an extremely effective decision-maker, if you're able to stay in the background and not deal with the office politics and drama or with clients and their many issues.

And because of your unemotional approach to work, others will not sway you with flattery or charm—you see right through it and will interpret it as inauthentic and manipulative, even when it may not be.

Self-Preservation Measures

You are very resourceful and feel content when you depend solely on yourself for the resources you need. In addition, you will seek out knowledge and facts to assist you in understanding things.

> And when life gets very stressful, withdrawing and isolating help
> you regroup and recharge.

As the reclusive Five, the expression "My home is my castle" is quite apropos! You require a private place where you can hide out, be quiet, think, assess, and analyse. You won't tolerate intrusions, interruptions, noise, too many questions or demands, or even frequent contact with others.

Your goal is to keep your life uncomplicated and simple because having many things in your life would simply slow you down, muddle your thinking, and feel burdensome. Other than having access to resources and knowledge, you don't value *things*.

In addition, you enjoy saving money and time, and you look for ways to save more of both. You don't want to be in debt and never consider loaning money to friends or family because you have worked too hard to squander your assets.

You rarely seek help from others or advice from friends. To you, it could be perceived as a sign of weakness, a chink in your self-reliant armour. And frankly, you do best to go within and reflect in private. The more time you spend with people, the less energy you have. It simply drains you to be around others!

In Relationships

Information plays a huge part in your relationships—whether you're sharing insider secrets with a co-worker, passing on some bit of gossip, speaking in a secret language you share only with your partner, or keeping things hush-hush in order to gain power over others and taking revenge on someone by not sharing key information. To you, information is leverage, and you use it to the hilt!

Because of your perception about information, you are adamant that your loved one not discuss your intimate relationship in public or share details of your personal business with others without getting your okay first.

You will rarely initiate discussions or conversations, but you do enjoy interesting talks that stimulate you mentally. You like to talk about practical matters, such as logistics, operations, systems, processes, scientific topics, mechanics, and how things function—or even more scholarly topics, such as arts, literature, and psychology.

> Despite your appearance of being distant and detached, you are quite involved with life; you're just more of an observer than a participator.

You feel more at ease watching than you do being a part of things. If you were put on the spot, you'd feel inept, inadequate, or uneducated. You particularly value people who respect your boundaries and honour your desire to stand back and observe.

You are able to understand your feelings best when you are alone and have the space to be reflective and thoughtful. It is at times like these that you become most clear about how you feel. The difficulty comes when you try to express yourself to your partner or friends—somehow the words have vanished, and you can't convey what was so clear to you earlier.

It's very helpful to express your feelings with actions or your senses. Being sensually intimate with your partner is key to you because you are able to express through your body (and get out of your head where your feelings don't make sense and get all jumbled).

Socially

Working on your own in a setting that you structure and control is the ideal environment for you. You enjoy being flexible and feeling like you are not being mandated to work a certain way.

> As a result, being self-employed or carving out your place in a large organization allows you to feel independent and in control.

It's no surprise then that policies, rules, and regulations tend to be bothersome to you. And meetings are something you avoid—unless you believe you can gather more knowledge or meet helpful people there. Since you enjoy learning from other experts in (and out of) your field, you will seek them out as resources of good information.

When your work output is good, you enjoy receiving praise from people you respect. You like a modicum of public attention for your insights and contributions, and you feel great fulfilment from having your work highlighted and your name respected—as long as the attention isn't overdone or too high profile. Despite this desire for recognition, you will not ask for it. You feel that it should be given simply because of the calibre of your output.

> Five's worldview: The world feels intrusive. I need time in private to think and re-energize.

Core Issues for Fives

Your biggest challenge comes from relying on thinking too much! You over-emphasize thinking and refrain from becoming involved in life. You miss out on participation, interaction, and connection with people and events. Your internal mental world is so engrossing that you exclude pretty much everything else from your life.

You are an observer on life—watching and noticing everything that goes on, taking it all in, and gathering information for future use. You are trying to understand the world outside of you by taking in enough data so that it will all make sense to you at some point. Thus, your focus is external.

> If you could confirm that your perceptions on the world are accurate, you would feel more confident putting yourself out into the experiences of the world.

The only thing you know for sure is what's inside your mind—your internal environment.

You feel insecure because the external environment is not predictable and feels threatening. You feel as if you have no ability to defend yourself, and you believe that you don't function as well as others do in navigating social realms. You also perceive your resources (time and energy) as finite; you will scale down your activities to keep them in line with your perceived quantity of resources. This creates a miserly attitude.

> Your growth will come from deciding to face your fears and stepping out into life, into the action.

By being less of an observer and taking a more active role in life, you will learn which of your perceptions are accurate and which aren't, you'll refine your observations and understanding about life, and you'll have a more balanced approach to living.

Sample Questions

- Have I pulled back from contact with others lately? Have I been isolating myself?
- How have I handled situations where I felt I was being intruded upon?
- Am I able to protect my boundaries in healthy ways?
- Have I tried to analyse situations in advance of experiencing them?
- When have I been a wallflower and watched from a distance?
- When is the last time I felt feelings and could stay connected to them in real-time (versus pushing them away until I was alone later and could reflect on them)?
- Am I aware of my wants and needs? Do I really want to be alone all the time?

The Core of Healing

- Be willing to experience your emotions as they come up, in the moment.
- Try to connect to people instead of retreating and isolating yourself.
- Begin to welcome more people into your close circle of friends and start building trusting relationships.
- Share yourself with others, express yourself in meaningful ways, and let others in.
- Get out into the world, participate in activities and events, and engage yourself.

Affirming Change

Affirmations, when used properly, are powerful tools for change. Affirmations are designed to speak directly to the subconscious mind and effect change on a level much deeper than your rational or conscious thoughts.

To use affirmations effectively, it's important to feel what you're saying and accept it as valid and real. Therefore, it's helpful to begin with an affirmation that allows you to release old beliefs and any thoughts that are no longer serving you. This is followed by a positive affirmation that brings in a new idea.

Begin by saying both affirmations. Once you feel comfortable saying the second affirmation, you can drop the first one and just use the second one:

- I release my feelings of being overwhelmed by others, the feeling of powerlessness, and my need to avoid by escaping into my mind.
- I trust that I am safe and secure in my life, and that the lessons of my past have come with many rewards. I now have faith in all of my tomorrows. I can create my reality. I am the power in my world.

Opportunities for Growth

Because of your analytical nature, it's important for you to start noticing when thinking and processing pull you out of your present experience. While your mental horsepower is an incredible gift, it can also be a weakness when you rely on it too much or use it as an escape from dealing with your emotions when they arise. Try to stay in your body and in touch with your feelings while you're in the experience. Remember that feelings do not always mean pain.

Start noticing when you feel emotions bubbling up—and pay attention to the times when you don't share them with others. It would also be helpful if you would observe the times when you withhold knowledge, energy, or time. A miserly attitude is not a flattering look on you!

Relaxing and chilling out are not things that come easily to you! Discover healthy ways to ramp down your energy without resorting to drugs or alcohol. Moving your body is a good idea, and any kind of exercise would be beneficial to you. Find something you enjoy, such as yoga, dancing, or jogging.

As the keenly perceptive Five, your abilities to scan and take in information are astounding! Unfortunately, you have difficulty choosing what to pay attention to and what is dross. By focusing on the gathering of data, you miss the bigger picture of what's really important.

> In order to learn how to assess the importance of information, try turning to a trusted advisor for his or her input.

Noticing how they make determinations of priority and importance will help you learn the skill as well. Another added benefit is that you'll begin to trust someone, which can be challenging for you.

Your awareness of all the potential problems with a relationship can become a self-fulfilling prophecy! Try to remember that conflict and disagreements are natural occurrences in relationships; the healthy way to resolve them is to work through them. Look for ways to resolve conflict instead of allowing yourself to withdraw and retreat into isolation.

Choose one or two close friends whom you trust enough to disagree with—and you may even tell them that you want to practice experiencing conflict. You might be surprised at how supportive they are of your change efforts!

Recognize that when you withdraw, you are forcing the other person to become active in coming to you. Start to understand that when you compartmentalize your relationships or withhold information from your partner or friends, you are trying to control the situation. Controlling and analysing are not good substitutes for feeling and connection!

Your curiosity about many subjects can take up much time and energy. Try to whittle down the list to a few topics that are the most interesting to you. Begin to observe yourself and watch when you are getting overinvolved in projects or trains of thought that aren't supportive of your self-confidence or that take too much of your time without much reward.

This is an area where you can begin to make decisions about what to weed out and what to pursue. By taking decisive action, you'll become more comfortable with the experience and will gain confidence in your ability and your perception.

> Your habit of minimizing your personal needs is not serving you, and it leaves you feeling alone and uncared for.

Begin sharing your needs with your mate and closest friends. For example, you might tell them how important private time is to you and that you need at least two hours a day by yourself to reflect and recharge. Once they understand why you retreat, they may become more supportive of you.

Because you are so intellectual, you may have attributed your withdrawal from feeling emotional pain as something desirable, similar to the concept of non-attachment found in spiritual studies, but it is not the same thing. Non-attachment means you are unattached to the outcome being one way or the other; in other words, you accept what is. But your unwillingness to feel your emotional pain is quite different—it's running away from life and rejecting what is.

As you become more involved in life's everyday activities and more connected with the people in your world, you won't feel so isolated and alone.

> Try being spontaneous and joining in without planning ahead.

You will still be able to fulfil your innate desire to observe, but your perspective will shift to observing you and your interactions with life and others as well.

Stages of Evolution

For every personality type, there are opportunities to live from several different stages of growth, depending on whether you are reflective and interested in growing or are happy with the status quo. In addition, not everyone who is a Five will have every trait or quality described here. Some will have traces of a characteristic, and others will see that same characteristic in abundance. A general overview of each stage is followed by a more detailed description.

Deteriorating

Seeking annihilation, wanting to be invisible, detached, may create an imaginary world, preoccupied with internal mental constructs, disconnected from reality, drawn to disturbing topics, intense, too much energy, fearful, overwhelmed, alone, lonely, unable to understand the world, retreating, nervous, restless, possibly hyperactive, may have insomnia, can't focus, scattered, compulsive, manic, antagonistic

When life feels overwhelming, you will retreat to your mind, to your inner sanctum, where everything makes sense and you feel safe and in charge. But as you know, you can't stay there forever! You need to come out and be a part of the world.

You have a tendency to be wound tightly and somewhat nervous; when you spend too much time in your mind, you are not expelling enough energy and your restlessness grows. You may turn to drugs or alcohol, develop insomnia, or get an ulcer or high blood pressure.

> In overdrive, your mind becomes less able to focus.

You feel scattered and anxious, jumping from one project to the next and never settling down for long. To others, you may appear manic or hyperactive. Your normally quiet nature changes, and you become talkative, compulsive, or antagonistic.

You may feel apathetic about everything, that nothing matters anymore, and become out of touch with any desires or dreams you once had. Achievement, which once stimulated you, may now feel like a burden. At the worst, you can become suicidal.

Status Quo

Withdrawn, feel intruded upon, cynical, detached, forceful, confrontational, provocative, controlling, disdainful, silent, preoccupied, impractical, easily distracted, feeling misunderstood, morose, confused by life, wallflower, focused, compulsively taking in information, feeling off balance, determined, compartmentalizes, distorts things, self-absorbed, eccentric, greedy, miserly

When the world barges in on you, which it frequently feels like it has, you batten down the hatches and go below. You hole up in your mind and withdraw with disdain. You may even stop speaking to others and give them the silent treatment.

If you're typically not confrontational, you may suddenly become assertive and argumentative, demanding your way. In your mind, taking control of the situation will help make you feel calmer and more confident about what will happen next. You are simply trying to reduce your mounting anxiety.

You can become preoccupied with many interests and projects—so much so that you neglect your partner and friends, and perhaps even your work. Being around other people, especially those you deem incompetent, is draining on you, and you find that escaping into your den provides solace.

The Alarm

When you become aware of your pattern of withdrawing from real-life experiences into the safety and comfort of your mind, your growth can begin. You've taught yourself that, by not needing anything from others, you can provide it all for yourself—and that everything can be found within your brain. But it's not true. The world is based on interdependence, and it's not possible to live a fulfilling, enriched life holed up in a room by yourself.

> Learning to engage in life and connect with others will help you
> come to a place of balance.

Evolving

Understands the world and how it works, connected to people, observant, analytical, satisfied, balanced, sees the truth of things, bigger perspective, innovative, perceptive, intelligent, wise, discerning with information, thoughtful, detailed, thorough, unique, kind, profound, expresses needs clearly

As you overcome your fear of being connected and engaged with the world, you feel less need for detachment and isolation. You begin to take in a bigger picture of life and to trust your own perceptions. The more you get out into the world and have experiences, the more self-confident you become. It's a positive cycle of growth.

Your intellectual capacities can be used in astounding ways, as you contribute unique, thoughtful, novel ideas at work and suggest new ways and methods that impress your employers. Since you're not afraid to speak up and share your ideas, your co-workers see you in a whole new light, a more flattering light.

The more positive feedback you receive, the more capable and confident you feel. The world is no longer a big, scary place! You feel grounded and at home when you're out in the thick of life.

> Socializing is becoming more comfortable, and you actually enjoy chatting with friends.

You are more in touch with your physicality and are comfortable with emotions as they occur. You take care of yourself and exercise regularly, eat healthy foods, and express your needs, wants, and feelings. Life feels easier.

On Your Spiritual Path

Original, insightful, broad perspective on life, comprehends world, profound understanding of processes of life, holistic view, contextual, pioneering, visionary, not attached to outcome, peaceful, embraces emotions, self-confident, humble, active, engaged in life, participatory, generous

The price you were paying for your self-imposed isolation became very apparent to you! You now connect deeply with others, have awareness of yourself and your emotions, and feel fully at home in the world.

You take on leadership roles and provide guidance and wisdom willingly. You seek responsibility and desire to contribute to society.

> You recognize the value of your perspective and insights and want
> to share them with others.

You have discovered that being of service in the world fulfils you. Your unassuming strength and quiet service do not go unnoticed; others seek you out for your compassionate nature and strong mentoring skills.

You've learned how to be a loving, accessible partner in an intimate relationship. And you feel at peace in the world, although you still enjoy some private time to go within and ponder big ideas, dream up new processes, and discover more depths to yourself.

You've learned that information is not all knowing, and that you can offer yourself to the world without worrying about being overwhelmed and annihilated. Through your growth, you've come to know how to live in a place of non-attachment and to experience the truth about life.

Type Five: The Agent

As the knowledgeable Five, your natural gifts are knowing what's going on, having the ability to gather and process large amounts of information, and being able to see things objectively. You like to think of yourself as scholarly and wise.

Secrecy is a way of feeling powerful for you, especially when it comes to timing the release of information to your best advantage. While you don't like to admit it, you enjoy controlling others indirectly by controlling access to data that they need or want.

Because you can retain so much information, you feel superior and different; you look down on those who don't have the resourceful brain that you have. You also believe that you are somehow not the same as everyone else. You feel misunderstood and find refuge in your mind.

You tend to separate yourself from society, from social gatherings, from large groups of people, and from the idle chitchat that others enjoy. In fact, you have found that compartmentalizing your life has helped you to muddle through, although you still don't really understand how life works.

As the expert Five, you are known for your depth of knowledge, breadth of expertise, and unparalleled perceptions and observations! Unfortunately, you don't feel this capability internally, and you fear being discovered as incompetent and inept.

> When you decide to stop hiding from life and begin to put yourself out into the world, you will begin to feel more confident and assured.

Each experience will add to your comfort level—until you make the shift and actually enjoy being engaged with people and life. When you do that, you will have taken the first step on your path to wholeness—and living a fulfilled life marked by rich relationships, inner peace, and using your remarkable talents to be of service to others. In other words, you will be an agent for change.

Type Six
The Patriot

I like to please others and make sure that they're okay.

I like to have the reassurance and support of others.

I constantly question myself about what might be wrong or what I've forgotten.

Reassure me that everything's okay.

Don't judge me for my anxiety.

I'm committed and faithful.

What am I supposed to do?

At my best I'm warm, playful, loyal, supportive, and reliable.

At my worst in a relationship, I can be suspicious, controlling, inflexible, and sarcastic. I also tend to withdraw.

I procrastinate so much that it's hard to make up my mind.

One of my biggest challenges is my deep-seated fear of abandonment.

6

Type Six—The Patriot

As Type Six (the Patriot), you want to be a part of the group, feel like you belong, and fit in. Feeling safe and sure and being able to trust the authorities in your life are important to you. Perhaps you have a valued belief system or cultural tradition that you put stock in. Whatever you choose to commit to, you are the most loyal of all the personality types.

You are dutiful, and you like to feel secure and certain. It's natural that you would enjoy being a follower and part of a group. Your friendly nature helps you get along with others. You want others to perceive you as dedicated, responsible, dependable, supportive, and loyal.

> You are not such an easy person to describe! You have many sides and ways of presenting yourself.

Sometimes you are cautious, anxious, and conservative; other times, you may rebel and feel brave and heroic. And depending on the situation you find yourself in and your mood at that moment, you can vacillate from outgoing and social to withdrawn and sceptical.

When a discussion comes up, you typically play the devil's advocate. And you are not one to seek out leadership roles because you fear becoming the target of those who would rebel against authority. Instead, you are drawn to strong, powerful, prestigious people you can trust and follow safely. You are an excellent friend, a loyal member of your family or community, a reliable employee, and a good soldier.

As someone who enjoys following a strong leader, you can empathize with the underdogs in any given situation. As a good listener, you hear everything and connect the dots in your mind, looking for how this information might affect others. Your attention to detail allows you to notice things that others miss. And justice is tantamount to you; many loyal Sixes work in the legal profession or as teachers or healers as a result of this inner drive for fairness and equality.

Especially drawn to those who are disadvantaged in some way (i.e. the elderly, children, the less fortunate), you naturally rise up to defend those whose voices are not normally heard. You have a natural insight into the problems that the underdog faces in life.

To the security-seeking Six, the world can be a very scary and unsafe place. By being loyal to protective authority figures and being a part of a group, you are creating a safe haven for yourself in the world.

> Be careful that you don't allow your worries about safety to make you suspicious and distrusting of people.

If this occurs, you may fear abandonment and head down the proverbial rabbit hole into acute anxiety or even paranoid schizophrenia.

Keep your focus in life positive; avoid negative thinking and doomsday predictions. You can trust your keen ability to ferret out people and organizations that are not on the up-and-up. If someone is inconsistent, you'll notice it because you tend to question any discrepancies you see. If someone passes your rigorous screening, they are trustworthy—and you can devote yourself to them safely.

In a Positive, Healthy State

As the responsible Six, you have a strong need to feel secure in life. The easiest way for you to feel safe is to be a part of a group and follow a leader you trust and respect. You are an ideal follower because you believe in allegiance and fealty over individuality. You work hard and are responsible; employers love you!

You have a wonderful curious nature, but sometimes it can make you suspicious and sceptical. You worry about not being prepared for every eventuality in life (which, of course, is not humanly possible!).

> You tend to run through scenarios in your mind, trying to scare yourself by thinking of the worst possible things that could happen.

Thinking the worst brings you comfort and helps you respond heroically when a crisis does occur. It makes you a great trouble-shooter who can foresee difficulties and issues before they occur.

When you allow yourself to release your doubts and fears, you feel excitement and anticipation instead of worry—and you have the uncanny ability to rise to the occasion and be quite unexpectedly courageous! And because you are very visual and creative, you may see what might go awry when others may not notice or be able to predict it. At your best, you are consistent, can rely on your own knowing, and can be a wonderful champion for others.

You feel best in predictable environments, around a reliable authority figure, and as part of a community or group. You look to the leader for guidance, and this helps you alleviate your fears and doubts. You trust a leader only after testing him or her thoroughly. You require proof that people, concepts, ideas, and organizations are worthy of your loyalty. And you enjoy receiving positive feedback, support, and reassurance from friends and family.

As the dedicated Six, you won't stray from the group's ideals or deviate from following their rules and norms. Disappointing others is not something you want to do! Despite your intense loyalty, you sometimes worry that you are too submissive. You may have moments of rebellion when you stand your ground and won't back down.

As a dedicated group member, you make sacrifices for the greater good and enforce the group's mores and tenets so that everyone is safe and sound.

> Your underlying belief is that if everyone followed the rules, the world would be safer.

Your incredible abilities to detect the truth and challenge unreliable authorities are your greatest assets. As you learn to relax a bit more in life and begin to trust your own knowing, your fears will transform into feelings of excitement and even bravery. If you can embrace the new and unknown aspects of life and trust what you know, you can become someone who takes action in life—and you can do so without following a proven authority.

In a Detrimental, Unhealthy State

Your greatest fear is of being abandoned, and this can cause you to feel sceptical of others and to distrust people in general. And while you desire to follow a strong leader, you question them at the same time.

Be careful where you place your focus. If you think too much about what can go wrong, what disasters might occur, or who might be plotting against you, you will begin an unhealthy downward spiral into a place of distrust, insecurity, anxiety, and overwhelming worry.

At your worst, you may set up an extremely rigid diet and avoid eating entire food groups, thus ending up nutritionally out of balance. You have a tendency towards workaholism, using caffeine and amphetamines to increase your endurance and give you energy, resorting to depressants and alcohol to numb your fears, and are more prone to alcoholism than most personality types.

You can be self-deprecating, furtive in your desire to continually look for danger, and may physically show signs of your heightened levels of fear and anxiety (i.e. verbal spewing, sweaty palms, panic attacks, outbursts at authority figures). Your habit of scanning the room to sense any potential danger, or to seek out people's hidden agendas, can cause paralysis and prevent you from taking action.

> Your overly phobic nature can cause you to not trust yourself and what you know.

While you have an incredible eye for details, if you're not careful, you may focus so much attention on the minutiae that you fail to see the big picture. In order to find solutions, you'll need to step back and put everything into its proper perspective.

You avoid anything that has not been proven or been around for a while. Deviating from the standard is not comfortable to you, and you are not likely to do anything that will make you stand out from your peers.

Your Achilles' heel is fear. Your fear of being alone and unprotected in the world may manifest as excessive anxiety, overwhelming doubt, or a need to test everyone and everything to prove that it's safe. You may picture the world as a dangerous place where you are being persecuted. In order to feel safe and make things orderly, you may begin to persecute others who aren't abiding by the group's rules of order.

When you are most afraid, you may doubt your own knowing and can act out, becoming devious, undermining, and even provocative. You may try to enlist others in your beliefs, fears, and worries. Your doubts about your own ability to lead can cause you to submit too much or rebel too much; you are unpredictable and can swing from one extreme to another.

Tips for Getting Along with Sixes

You might want to share some important points with close friends, family, and those with whom you work closely. These ideas may help others understand you better and teach them how best to interact with the trustworthy Six.

You have a habit of questioning people's motives and hidden agendas; your friends and family should be direct with you and state things clearly. They will want to listen carefully to you and help you work things through in your mind. Reassurances from your partner will go a long way towards making you feel safe and comfortable with regard to your relationship.

> You enjoy laughing, and friends can help you lighten up and see the comical side of things.

Friends can encourage you to experience new things and stretch yourself a little. You are so worried about disappointing others that your friends and family will want to avoid judging you or even appearing to judge you. If they can refrain from reacting to you when you overreact, it will help you calm down.

You are a most loyal friend; as such, you expect the same from your friends. You hang onto relationships longer than most people do and are fiercely defensive of your family and loved ones, standing up for them even more than for yourself. You do this because of your intense fear of abandonment. As a result, it would take a lot for you to abandon a loved one.

You rely on your social network to help you deal with life because you worry that you cannot handle the challenges of life on your own. You perceive your loved ones and close friends as crucial to your very survival! You work hard to develop and sustain strong connections.

Because it takes you so long to overcome your distrust, to prove to yourself that something is worth believing in, and then to adopt a belief, it would be quite damaging for your friends to question your beliefs or challenge you to give them up. In addition, once you have vetted a friend and decided that he or she is trustworthy, you will rely on that friend as a resource for guidance, advice, mentoring, and emotional support. You will not let go of that relationship easily or whimsically.

Admirable Qualities of a Six

As the faithful Six, you are committed to your friends and loved ones. They can count on you to defend them, have their backs, and be fiercely loyal to them for life. You are not a fickle friend by any means.

> You are one of the trustworthiest and hardest-working employees around!

Your boss and co-workers can count on you to take responsibility and deliver on your promises. Your intelligence and sense of humour make it easy to work alongside you, and people enjoy having you on the team.

Despite your desire to appease authority figures, you also have a nonconformist, rebellious streak running through you! When push comes to shove, you are a brave, heroic sort who will confront danger without flinching. You are the one to rescue the cat from the tree, clear the burning building, and stand up to a bully in defence of a friend.

You're not afraid to be direct in your approach to others, to say what's on your mind, or to tell it like it is. Despite your assertive manner, you are very compassionate and caring. You find it easy to put yourself in another's shoes and understand how they might feel, especially an underdog.

Pressures and Limitations

Making decisions can be challenging for you because there is a continual back-and-forth process for you. As a result, you may find yourself procrastinating rather than making a decision. Just remember that making no decision is still a decision!

> Procrastination is often due to a fear of failure or of being seen as inadequate or lacking knowledge.

Sometimes you don't have much self-confidence, and this is one way you express that self-doubt.

You may wish you had written rules at work that spelled out every possible scenario and what to do in order to execute things successfully; this would make life easy for you. You are great at following the rules! Since no such thing exists, you become exhausted and worn out from trying to figure out the right way to do everything.

You can also be overly critical of yourself, demanding too much and expecting super-human accomplishments. This occurs especially when you feel that you have let yourself down or haven't met your own requirements for perfection.

The biggest challenge is your deep-seated fear of abandonment, which can be evidenced in many ways, including worrying that you might be taken advantage of, that someone might pull the wool over your eyes, or that you may be taken in and fooled. Any type of betrayal, no matter how small, feels like you have been abandoned—and that is the most frightening feeling you know.

As Children

You may recall being very friendly and outgoing as a child. You were likeable and had many friends. People could rely on you; even as a child, you were the dependable Six. Sometimes you may have gotten a bit big for your britches and acted bossy, obstinate, or sarcastic.

As the hyper-vigilant Six, you were always on the lookout for danger, which left you feeling anxious and worried. Even at a young age, you looked to your social network to help you feel safer in the world.

> You may have banded with others in an us-versus-them attitude on the playground or with a parent.

You perceived authority figures and organizations as mechanisms for support as well. You felt safe and protected when you were a part of something bigger and grander than yourself. Despite this loyalty, you still felt the need to rebel occasionally, to make a stand for yourself, and to question authority's right to rule the way they did.

For many Sixes, there's a strong possibility that you've come from an abusive childhood where you experienced emotional or physical abuse, neglect, and abandonment of some type. This helps you understand where your intense fear of abandonment as an adult stems from.

You may have lived with an alcoholic parent or an emotionally unpredictable parent. Since you are so dependable and compassionate, you probably took on the burden of your parent's emotions and frailties, carrying their fear and anxiety as if it were your own.

As Parents

> Sixes tend to be loving, caring, empathetic parents with a strong sense of obligation and parental responsibility.

You are nurturing but can overdo it at times; you may find occasions when you are hesitant to allow your children the independence needed to blossom.

Your worrying nature extends to your children, and you probably spend more time than most parents do worrying about your children's safety and possible harm that may come to them. As a result of this, you may overindulge your children, have trouble defining clear boundaries and enforcing them, and find it difficult to say no to your kids.

Tips for Living with Sixes

In Love

You are a loyal partner and a dedicated supporter. You think of your relationship as an us-against-the-world duo. Despite your deep, fierce devotion, you will question your mate's intentions, wonder what they're really thinking or feeling, worry if their expressions are authentic, and devalue their attempts at being romantic.

You need a great deal of reassurance to help you get past all these worries—even if they're completely unfounded. Your biggest concern is if your partner will always love you; unfortunately, there is no answer they can give that will satisfy you! Even if they assure you that they will always love you, you doubt their sincerity and require even greater assurances to assuage your fragile heart.

As a visual Six, you may have a wandering eye that enjoys looking at other attractive people. But if your partner calls your attention to your behaviour, you will feign dissatisfaction with your mate for the exact same reason in an attempt to take the focus off of yourself and your obvious misbehaviour.

You'll need to be careful about your tendency to focus on the negatives in your relationship. If you don't make efforts to notice the positives, you can convince yourself that your partnership is doomed.

> If there is real tension in your relationship, you are not the one who can identify the cause or contributing factors.

You are unwilling to be vulnerable and let your guard down long enough to really look at yourself in any kind of objective light. It's just too scary for you since it brings up your fear of abandonment if your mate ever found out what you're really like.

Instead, you will look to your loved one's behaviour for clues about what's wrong. The cause of the problem will always be found in *his or her* behaviour—never in yours. And you are quick to come to conclusions, sometimes wrong, based on what you observe in this behaviour. You will need further reassurance that your relationship is not in danger of dissolving.

In order to feel as though you are in control of the relationship and are keeping your heart safe, you will want to be the one to emotionally affect your partner (rather than vice versa). In other words, you would rather convey deep emotions or sexual desire to your partner than be the one receiving those messages. Being on the receiving end makes you feel too vulnerable and unsafe.

You love to help others achieve their goals and are a very supportive partner in that regard. You are even capable of extreme self-sacrifice, all in the interests of maintaining the relationship and keeping your mate from deserting you.

Decision-making can become tense in your relationship; although you have a difficult time making up your mind, you certainly don't want anyone else to tell you what to do! You do not want to feel controlled—even by someone you love.

You may choose to remain in an unhappy relationship because you feel supported and safe when you have someone by your side. The thought of being on your own (me against the world) terrifies you!

Until you are ready to end the relationship (most likely because you found a replacement partner), you will bend over backwards to make your mate happy enough so that they won't leave you.

In the Workplace

As the analytical Six, you are a force to be reckoned with! Your natural doubts and suspicions about whatever is being presented or sold cause you to question the opposite approach, play the devil's advocate, and look for flaws.

You have an uncanny ability to punch holes in someone's position, find the weak spots in the case, and bring up the opposing viewpoint in order to gain an objective, balanced perspective on the situation.

Another of your attributes is your ability to take action even when you're up against the wall or when the odds aren't in your favour. You love an unbalanced competition and will root for the underdog every time. You're a great asset to have in a business turnaround situation.

You have a tendency to project too much power onto authority figures, imbuing them with more power than they really have and causing you to feel weaker in comparison. When you're feeling weak, you seek out the protection of someone more powerful or attempt to bring down the powers-that-be. You are all or nothing—totally loyal or leading the rebellion!

You have a constant undertow of internal anxiety, and one of your strategies for diminishing it is to try to be a superstar or a hero in order to prove yourself. You believe that if you can master yourself, overcome the odds, face the fear, and save the day, you will finally prove to yourself how valuable and worthwhile you are.

When you experience success, you may find it challenging to keep your progress in motion. It's hard for you to focus when there is no opposing force to overcome! You may experience doubt that a positive outcome is even possible.

> You may become paralysed by your anxiety and not be able to take any action— even when you're so close to achieving your goal.

Should you still happen to achieve success, you may play it down, do something to sabotage yourself or the project, lose the file, crash your computer, or just blow it in general. Success brings out a feeling of vulnerability that is quite uncomfortable to you; it almost feels as if you're in danger of being seen, being noticed, and possibly being held accountable.

In the back of your mind, it's not safe to become too successful and move up to a leadership position because you would be in the line of fire for any backlash or rebellions that arise. Your firm belief is that nobody likes authority figures.

You may not fully understand all the dynamics that arise within you when success pops up its head. There is an undercurrent of tension and worry, and you may begin to think that people are plotting to undermine you, that others are rebelling against your position or direction, or that people are out to get you in general.

> Your overall feeling about success is one of concern and fretting; you simply don't understand why you aren't enjoying it!

Self-Preservation Measures

As the warm and ingratiating Six, you really want people to like you and accept you because that helps you feel safe and secure. In return, you look for any chance you can find to show your loyalty and devotion to your friends (and you certainly expect them to do the same for you).

Your responsible nature enables you to astutely assess how those in authority see you, and this ability helps you stay on their good sides (or if you've fallen out of favour, to realize it and work to get back in favour).

Your desire to please others can cause you to be untrue to your own emotions. For example, even if you're angry, you may act friendly and as if all is well. You don't want to take a chance that you might upset someone! You tend to worry and fret more than most, and you look to others for much-needed reassurance and support.

You may have heard people refer to your behaviour as "paralysis by analysis." You will examine and weigh every possible outcome of an action before you take it. You want to be certain that you won't make a mistake or put yourself in any type of danger (either physical or social).

Since staying safe is so important to your mental and emotional well-being, you need to live in a home that is secure and makes you feel protected and cocooned away from the dangers of the world.

In Relationships

You are the strong Six and work earnestly to accomplish your goals. You can be quite competitive in relationships and have a great deal of energy to funnel into them. You enjoy keeping your body and mind strong, and it's equally important to you that you appear attractive to others (both sexually and aesthetically).

> You want to feel as though others know you and care about you, and you expect them to help you when you need it!

Your personality type is likely to take classes in self-defence or martial arts because you want to know that you are capable of taking care of yourself and defending yourself if the need arises.

Male Sixes tend to put themselves in situations that they are afraid of in an effort to overcome their fears. In addition, all Sixes will seek to build strong social networks so that you have a web of support to fall back on, should you ever need it. But no matter how strong your support network is, you may still feel an undercurrent of fear and uneasiness, an anxiety you just can't put your finger on.

You are quite dependent upon your friends' opinions and like to check in with them for approval, especially those whom you see as authorities. Since you can be affected by outside influences more than most, be careful not to become like a tennis ball, being lobbed back and forth between competing advice-givers and never making a decision of your own. In order to grow, you will need to learn to trust your own mind and your own judgments.

> You are a tough cookie to pin down since you can vacillate between the extremes in your behaviour.

Sometimes you are overly dependent, and other times you are fiercely independent. Sometimes you are argumentative, and other times you are too conciliatory. Sometimes you are cooperative and obedient to authority, and other times you are leading the rebellion!

It is this unpredictable nature of yours that is a defining quality of the Six. You are impossible to pin down since you exhibit the black and the white aspects of each quality you possess.

In your close relationships, you will find your unresolved emotional insecurities being poked and prodded, and this will probably feel quite uncomfortable. In reaction to this discomfort, you will try to create a safe environment (in whatever way makes sense to you).

The problem is that the world is in a constant state of flux, and it is not possible for you to foresee every possible danger and prepare for them all. Instead of warding off danger, you will need to learn to face your fears and anxieties if you ever hope to feel safe and happy in an intimate relationship.

Socially

Everyone who has ever been a significant authority figure in your life has taken up residence in your head! When you need to make a decision, large or small, you consult this panel of experts to ensure that you are not making a mistake.

With your unpredictable responses to situations, you will be concerned about following the rules of a group—or you'll be the one conspiring with others to break them. You'll be happy to be told what to do by those in authority—or you'll be annoyed at being bossed around.

You are known for your loyal and dependable behaviour when it comes to family and friends, although you are quite sceptical of strangers and those you don't know yet. And you've come to believe that you can't rely on any one person because that is too risky. Instead, you trust groups or causes for the support you so desperately need. When it comes to success, you are in a conundrum! You truly want to succeed, but you are afraid of being promoted.

You worry that if you are in a highly visible, responsible role, other people will poke fun at you, criticize you, or try to bring you down (just as you do with your superiors).

Part of what causes you to fluctuate in how you perceive authority figures is your tendency to first idolize and idealize your boss and then later feel completely disillusioned and frustrated with that same leader. When you are able to see people in their wholeness (both the good and the bad), you will find a better balance for your views of those in authority.

The devoted Six is the one any cause or charity will want working for them! You will contribute endless hours and energy to a cause or effort that you believe in. Who wouldn't want such a trooper on their team?

> Six's worldview: I have to question authority because the world is a dangerous place.

Core Issues for Sixes

As the wary Six, you see the world as an unsafe, unpredictable, dangerous place. In your efforts to control your environment and feel more certain about your safety and protection, you try to avoid any perceived danger by being hyper-vigilant, questioning everyone's motives, and overcoming perilous hazards.

In the process, you wrestle with your anxiety, fear, and doubts. You worry about the never-ending questions about your security and your imaginative projections of worst-case scenarios and how you'll handle them. And along the way, you lose sight of the basic tenet that you can trust and have faith in yourself, in others, and in life.

Your inability to feel an underlying sense of safety in the world, coupled with your intense fear and anxiety, cause you to ricochet from one emotional state to another. It may appear to others as though you are unstable, unpredictable, and full of contradictions.

> In an attempt to stabilize yourself, you seek out solid organizations, causes, beliefs, companies, and authority figures.

Since you don't really trust solid structures, your vacillating cycle begins again.

In order for you to grow, become more stable as a personality, and more consistent in your psychological state, you must regain faith and trust in yourself, in others, and in the universe. And you will need to do this without any proof that your faith is warranted!

Begin to face the scenarios that frighten you and draw on your innate courage to walk through the fear and out the other side.

> Resist your natural tendency to back away from the fear or to challenge it to a duel! Neither of those paths will work (or have worked) for you.

Your growth path is to move through the fear and doubt, to trust what you know about how to handle life's various situations, and to realize that you don't have to keep proving yourself to yourself or to the world. By doing this, you will come to a place of being able to live comfortably with uncertainty.

Sample Questions

- What causes me to become panicked, alarmed, or fearful?
- What did I avoid or challenge when I was afraid?
- Am I magnifying things and giving them worst-case spins?
- What am I projecting onto external situations?
- Have I doubted my internal thought process? When was I playing devil's advocate?
- Have I been on the fence or ambivalent about decisions?

The Core of Healing

- Recognize that insecurity is just a part of living—and give up the need for certainty. It is simply a substitute for having faith in yourself and life.
- Work at differentiating between true impressions and your skewed interpretations.
- Understand that both ends of the spectrum of your behaviour are the result of your response to fear. Learn to welcome your fear, subdue it, and move ahead in spite of it.
- Notice when you put a negative interpretation on things—and change it to a more positive outlook.

- Become your own authority and develop faith in yourself, others, and the world.

Affirming Change

Affirmations, when used properly, are powerful tools for change. Affirmations are designed to speak directly to the subconscious mind and effect change on a level much deeper than your rational or conscious thoughts.

To use affirmations effectively, it's important to feel what you're saying and accept it as valid and real. Therefore, it's helpful to begin with an affirmation that allows you to release old beliefs and any thoughts that are no longer serving you. This is followed by a positive affirmation that brings in a new idea.

Begin by saying both affirmations. Once you feel comfortable saying the second affirmation, you can drop the first one and just use the second one:

- I release my self-punishing tendencies, anxieties, and fears of being abandoned and alone. I let go of my feelings of inferiority and my need to look to others to make me feel secure.
- I now choose to have faith in myself, my talents, and all that I have to offer. I am safe and secure in all I do. I can truly say that I am the power in my world.

Opportunities for Growth

One of the best ways you can change your thinking is to give yourself regular reality checks. Question whether your doubts and fears are based in reality or in your internal perceptions of reality. Begin to label your fears and learn to identify them. You may even want to ask a trusted friend for feedback as you practice this new way of being.

Everyone needs a support system, but for the dutiful Six, it is an absolute necessity! Share your change efforts with your close friends and seek out encouragement and feedback as you grow and change. Build your network of trustworthy people and allow yourself to become close to those friends. This is a risky move on your part and may cause you to feel even more fearful, but it's important to connect and commit to your relationships. Begin to let your closest friends and your partner know how you feel about them.

Be cautious not to enter into vague or nebulous agreements or contracts. You need very clear parameters and detailed step-by-step actions to take so that you can rely on these clear guidelines should your fear kick in. In this way, you can move through the fear instead of shying away from it or magnifying its importance.

Begin to identify your fight-or-flight tendencies. Watch for distorted interpretations or dysfunctional projections when you perceive others as hostile or undermining.

Learn to give equal attention to positive impressions and look for alternative positive ways of perceiving people and scenarios.

Manage your procrastination by following timelines and having checklists of what tasks need to be completed by when. And notice when you spend too much time thinking and not enough time taking action. You can catch yourself sooner and sooner, until you are free of the habit of procrastinating.

If you find yourself fixated on negative outcomes or worst-case possibilities, flip your perception on its head; in other words, see the exact opposite as possible outcomes (see the positive). Try exaggerating the worst-case scenario until it appears ludicrous! These mental tricks will help you get unstuck and move on with a more positive outlook.

Recognize that there is nothing wrong with feeling some anxiety because everyone does at one time or another. Become very present and aware of your anxious feelings, learn to delve into them, and come to a place of peace with them. Learn to be creative in handling your fears instead of resorting to excessive use of alcohol or drugs. You may even find that your anxiety can be turned into positive energy to help you become more productive and aware!

Be careful when you are upset or on edge since you may take it out on others and blame them for things you have done. Notice your own pessimism, darkness, and negative thinking, and how you project this onto your external world.

You can be your own worst enemy if you allow your doubts and fears to rule you.

If you are stressed or anxious, you may find yourself overreacting. Start to figure out what caused you to overreact. You may even review your life and see that none of the things you so feared in the past ever actually came true! Even when things are bad, your negativity weakens your constitution and keeps you from making positive changes in your life. Learn to manage your internal mindset and keep it in a positive frame of reference.

Understand that your perceptions of people are much worse than the truth of the matter. People most likely think more highly of you than you imagine they do. Realize that your fears about what others think about you actually indicate what *you* think about you and how you view others!

As the questioning Six, use your natural ability and curiosity to ferret out what's real in the world and to differentiate that from your internal perceptions and interpretations. As you do, you will begin to recognize when your impressions are off base and when they are sound; in the end, you'll learn to trust yourself more.

Stages of Evolution

For every personality type, there are opportunities to live from several different stages of growth, depending on whether you are reflective and interested in growing or are happy with the status quo. In addition, not everyone who is a Six will have every trait or quality described here. Some will have traces of a characteristic, and others will see that same characteristic in abundance. A general overview of each stage is followed by a more detailed description.

Deteriorating

Indecisive, project blame, rebellious, vacillating between emotional states, too dependent, too independent, overly focused on authority figures, paranoid, fearful, anxious, doubt-filled, committed, curious, cautious, devoted, dutiful, unpredictable, blustery, assertive, withdrawn, fear abandonment, distrusting, suspicious, unsafe, nervous, self-doubting, think obsessively, procrastinating, hard-working, feel inadequate and inferior, self-disparaging, defenceless, overwhelmed, task-focused, hysterical, paranoid, irrational, violent

When you feel overwhelmed by life, you become agitated, nervous, and anxious. You will react to situations with self-doubt and tend to think too much about everything before taking action. You may even become paralysed by analysis and procrastinate about making a decision.

If your fears take you beyond your normal stress level, you might throw yourself into your work, trying to become more efficient and more task-focused than ever before. This frenzied expression of your energy helps dispel the built-up tension and mounting anxiety you have been feeling, and it helps you avoid your feelings of inadequacy.

You certainly don't want anyone else to know how overwhelmed you are by everything! You put on a mask of having it all handled and being on top of things.

> Unfortunately, when you get to this state, you are no longer in touch with your feelings (if you were, you wouldn't be able to continue to function).

This can lead to serious difficulties with your close relationships and with your emotional stability. You might lash out at, berate, blame, or disparage others in an effort to feel better about yourself.

At your worst, you can be manic, over-responsible, impulsive, imprudent, risk-taking, and frenzied with overdoing things. This is a masochistic way for you to try to (ineffectively) manage your anxieties. Excessive use of alcohol, drugs, and self-mutilating behaviours are possible.

Feelings of persecution and paranoia grow, and you lash out at the world in an effort to protect yourself. And if you allow yourself to spiral downward, you can become self-destructive, violent, or suicidal.

Status Quo

Follow the rules, worried, good friend, cautious, obedient, responsible, permission-seeking, uncertain, efficient, dedicated, friendly, dependable, reactive, passive-aggressive, evasive, procrastinating, negative, contradictory, confused, seek out authority, need certainty, hyper-vigilant, focused on safety, doubting, continually questioning, scanning, threatened, untrusting

Feeling quite insecure about life, you may be sarcastic or tough on strangers, look to blame others when things go wrong (including in your intimate relationship), or become very defensive and over-reactive. You are on the alert for threats and danger at all times, and you may see people as either friends or enemies, with no middle ground.

While you seek out authority figures to follow, you resent their power and are fearful of them and are suspicious about their hidden agendas. You may even become the leader of a rebellious coup!

> You tend to be passive-aggressive, fluctuating from one extreme to another.

You can be evasive, procrastinating, and uncertain one moment and appear to be confident, dependable, and responsible the next. No one knows who they'll meet when they greet you each day.

The mixed signals you give off create confusion in those who are trying to interact with you—and within yourself. You don't even know how you'll respond to the next situation! Your constant vigilance and worries about impending problems keep you on high alert (which is a stressful way to live on a daily basis!).

One coping technique is to shut down and stop caring about your environment and what's going on around you. When you are no longer bothered or upset by the occurrences in your world, you feel a temporary respite from the overwhelming pressure.

> Your interpersonal relationships suffer; you come across friendly and kind one moment and stubborn and withdrawn the next.

At this stage, you perceive requests from friends and loved ones as untoward demands on you, and you respond by being spiteful or passive-aggressive towards them. You may even become so pulled-in and internalized that you stop responding to others at all, and you just try to go through the motions of your mind-numbing routines.

The Alarm

When you become aware of how dependent you are on outside influences to guide your every decision, you can begin to go within, learn how to trust your inner knowing, and feel faith in yourself and your abilities. When you stop looking to authority figures for answers, you'll be able to let go of your distrust. You will learn to trust your inner guidance to steer you on the path that's right for you, and you'll find that the support you so desperately needed from social networks will come from inside!

Evolving

Interdependent, good friend, faithful, trusting, has faith in others, responsible, committed, feels safe and secure in the world, dependable, trustworthy, loyal, in touch with self, reaches out to others, caring, concerned, courageous, calm, warm, affectionate, balanced, engaging, supportive, organized, dedicated, involved in community, reliable, cooperative, appealing, able to bond with others, lovable

As you evolve and grow, you are able to connect deeply with others, stay present to them and their needs without feeling burdened, and remain centred in your heart. You are a very dedicated and loyal friend, and you are willing to help out and take on responsibility.

You enjoy participating in community activities, supporting others' wishes and goals, and most likely are a strong contributor towards a cause or movement. You seek out organizations in which to invest your time and resources—ones that make you feel good about what they're doing and accomplishing.

You now feel safe in the world and it shows! Your former hyper-vigilance has calmed down and is now at a normal level of awareness.

> You are a natural at building alliances and forming cooperative connections.

You feel good about yourself and are able to see others the way they really are, instead of through your formerly distorted lens. People can trust you because you no longer vacillate wildly and have a steady presence and manner. As such, others are drawn to your endearing qualities.

On Your Spiritual Path

Trusting, believing, understanding, caring, compassionate, self-affirming, see others as equals, courageous, positive thinking, strong leader, fully expressive, affectionate, open, interested, brave, peaceful, serene, tuned into inner knowing, feel supported, confident, believe in self

After living in a world that was fraught with peril at every turn, where you felt unsafe, uncertain, anxious, and worried, you realized there had to be a better way! And now you've found it.

You trust yourself implicitly and know how to access your inner guidance and intuition about what's right for you. You have found security and support in the world, and it is within you. Trusting and believing in yourself has proven to be the greatest balm for what ailed you.

You are able to remain calm, serene, and courageous in any circumstance life dishes up because you have an inner sense of peace no matter what is going on externally. Your hyper-vigilance has transformed into a healthy ability to notice and spot potential problems that others might miss—but now you do so without the overwhelming worry and fear.

Since you no longer feel put upon by others' needs or requests, you have become a thoughtful and considerate person who is intuitive about what others are feeling. You are interdependent, yet still quite independent when it's appropriate, and able to be cooperative when that is called for.

All these traits have naturally pushed you into a leadership position (whether formal or informal), and you feel at ease in this role. You are no longer afraid of being an authority.

> You find it rewarding to model the hard-won lessons you've learned
> and mastered in life.

Type Six: The Patriot

As the friendly Six, you have a natural care and concern for any group or organization you belong to. You are dependable and reliable unless you get upset with authority; you can fluctuate greatly in your behaviour and manners. There may be times when you challenge authority figures and rebel against them. People are not sure how to take you because of this all-or-nothing behaviour!

You are extremely aware of potential danger or threats to your safety and security, and you have intense worry and anxiety as a result. Your suspicious nature and negative thoughts erode your own sense of well-being in the world.

Making decisions can be gut wrenching for you and can cause you to procrastinate or have insomnia. It's much easier for you to align yourself with a strong, powerful authority figure or become a part of a bigger group so that you can go along and not have to be held responsible for choosing directions or offering ideas.

As you grow and learn about yourself, you discover that all the security you need can be found deep within you.

Once you figure this out, you are able to blossom into your fuller self. When this occurs, you no longer predict the worst, feel burdened by life, or are afraid of every shadow. You begin to emerge from your cocoon and step into your true self.

Trusting yourself and being in touch with your inner voice will allow you to open up to whatever life brings, to be present with others and their feelings, and to have a deeper acceptance of the ups and downs of everyday life. You will begin to include others in your life and be able to offer support because you will have the energy and positive concern for others that you were lacking before.

You will learn how to quiet your mind and cease its endless ruminating so that your inner wisdom can speak to you clearly. As a result, you'll feel stable, safe, connected, peaceful, and happy. You'll be able to be a community organizer, a champion of others, and a true patriot in the world.

I'm generous and look for ways to help others and make the world a better place.

Tell me that you appreciate my incredible vision and inspiring new ideas.

I love that I'm optimistic, spontaneous, and free-spirited.

Others are drawn to me when I'm positive and upbeat.

Type Seven
The Aficionado

I dislike being confined or held back.

I have so much I want to do and achieve.

I love to be stimulated, excited, and engaged.

At my best I'm outgoing, caring, generous, fun, and light-hearted.

At my worst in a relationship, I can be defensive, distracted, opinionated, and narcissistic, especially if I feel held back.

I fear failure and not being able to handle my inner emotions.

My world is full of opportunities and possibilities. I look forward to new adventures.

7

Type Seven—The Aficionado

As Type Seven (the Aficionado), you enjoy a good time and look for every opportunity to explore new experiences, have new adventures, and meet new people. You are quite spontaneous and are known to change course in mid-stream if something more appealing shows up. You see the world as filled with an endless array of options, and you find it hard to choose just one at a time.

Happiness is your goal, and you enthusiastically pursue it with a head full of optimistic thinking. You need to be stimulated, excited, and engaged. You enjoy feeling creative, playful, and fascinated with life. As the outgoing Seven, you seek out the new, the untried, and the unusual.

You imagine yourself to be quite the visionary, and you hope that others perceive you as fascinating, intriguing, and fun. Life needs to be interesting, varied, happy, and joyful for you to feel satiated and fulfilled.

> People are fascinating to you, and you know how to charm them all.

Your positive, upbeat attitude is a bright light to some people's dreary days. Your optimism and quick humour entertain and inspire others. If you had your way, you would spread your ideas of love, freedom, and equality around the world.

Because of this high-energy drive for lots of variety and novelty, you can be scattered, distractible, and even frenzied at times. The good side of this interest in so many things is that you are the true jack-of-all-trades with a breadth of skills and experiences.

Your attention tends to focus on one main subject: you. The world is viewed through the lens of what affects you, what concerns you, what you are thinking, planning, and doing, what your options are, and the importance of your vision being more relevant than that of others.

In order to feel free to pursue your many interests, you need to feel untethered and free. Your creative nature feels eternally youthful and playful, much like the whimsical nature of a child. To you, feeling loved means you are getting your way and being indulged.

> Delusions of grandeur are common to your personality type, and you may have a know-it-all attitude.

It's hard for you to stay committed to a person or project because there is always something new coming around the next bend. Since you enjoy all kinds of people without regard to status or power, distractions are everywhere.

When dealing with authority, instead of going against the grain, you are adept at finding your way around the rules. You may find it challenging to be held accountable or responsible, and you'll use your quick thinking and charming smile to find a way around most things you find unpleasant. As the versatile Seven, you can talk your way out of anything!

You have an innate ability to think in new ways, envision new possibilities, and enjoy a life filled with joy and abundance. Your loving, generous nature takes people's minds off of their troubles. You enjoy passing out happiness in small or large doses to anyone who needs it, and you make it your goal to add fun to people's lives.

It's important to remember to follow your heart because it will guide you to the most rewarding experiences and opportunities. Living in the magical world of your imagination allows you to create new ideas and ensures that even mundane activities are magical adventures!

In a Positive, Healthy State

As the fun-loving Seven, you love nothing more than exploring what the world has to offer, and you relish your feelings of appreciation and happiness. You are the most adaptable of the personality types and have been known to turn a bad situation around so that it will benefit you somehow.

Your plans must remain changeable, open-ended, and fluid so you can turn on a moment's notice in search of some new experience. Being in the flow of life feels good to you.

> You won't enjoy being tied down to a plan or schedule.

And just like your plans, your mind is versatile and malleable. You are ready with innovative ideas and solutions, and you are able to think quickly on your feet. And while you won't be concerned with being right, it is important to you to win (even if you're wrong).

Your creative mind is great at coming up with out-of-the-box ideas, trying approaches that others scoff at as silly or unlikely, and inventing new ways to do things. You are not happy with the simple answer and want to explore all the angles until you understand the problem in its entirety.

Your ability to assess all the underlying issues quickly and deftly leaves co-workers dumbfounded. You often assess things in a fresh, insightful manner. Once you grasp the complexity of a situation, you are clear and decisive in solving it. Few others have your ability to find solutions to challenging problems!

To you, quality is more important than quantity. Your perfectionist nature can become easily annoyed when co-workers want to cut corners. This is one of the times when you may feel superior to others since you have more patience than most in staying focused on a quality outcome.

In order to avoid feeling bored or anxious, you will fill your days with diverse, exciting activities, people, and ideas. To the energetic Seven, life is one huge adventure just waiting to be discovered!

In a Detrimental, Unhealthy State

If you are unable to satiate your need for exploration and variety, you can become bored, miserable, and restless. Your focus may turn even more on you as you try to find a way to avoid the sadness and emotional pain. If you feel stifled or trapped, it will trigger one of your deepest fears: that you may be missing out on something.

Any type of limitation or restriction on you feels painful and confining. You don't want to feel incomplete or unfulfilled. When you start to feel this way, you may find yourself indulging in all kinds of pleasures, acting like a kid in a candy store, or running wild from one hedonistic experience to the next. Your personality type is the most likely to develop addictions, especially to stimulants (amphetamines, cocaine, caffeine), narcotics, alcohol, and psychotropics.

Because you have a shallow view of life (flitting from flower to flower), you assume others do as well. You may minimize the facts about a situation or trivialize emotional concepts like love, truth, and the meaning of life. You might even resort to scamming or swindling people in order to win at all costs.

Be careful that you don't become too critical of others and judge them for the very things you dislike in yourself: the excesses, self-indulgences, and extremes. Despite your superior attitude at times, you secretly worry that you are not as valuable or as smart as others are. You lack self-confidence and want to be noticed. You try to stay as positive and upbeat as possible because you know that others are drawn to you when you are.

Feeling inferior is very uncomfortable for you.

Most painful emotions are overwhelming to you, and you avoid discussing them or sharing them with anyone. You make a concerted effort to stay away from negative people because you fear they will bring you down to their levels. As a result of all of this avoidance, you may not live in the present moment; you might enjoy an internal fantasy world that is based upon all your future dreams and visions.

In your attempt to convince everyone of your positive, fascinating attitude towards life, you may come across as condescending, frenzied, loud, or egotistical. Those who don't care for your approach to life might describe you as having a short attention span, always looking for the next big thing, moving way too fast, or being too loose with the truth.

Your downfall is overdoing things, indulging in excesses, and pursuing stimulating experiences until you become physically ill from exhaustion. If you don't manifest your dreams (see them through to conclusion), you can become cynical, jaded, greedy, or selfish. If your dreams go unmet, your self-indulgences can escalate to epic proportions, and you may stop caring about following through, meeting commitments, and keeping your word.

You have a secret fear of not being able to handle your inner world, your feelings, and your pain. You may resort to coping by escaping to the external world of activities, people, and things. This feels like a safe way to avoid dealing with yourself, but as you know, we all have to come home and face ourselves eventually.

Tips for Getting Along with Sevens

You might want to share some important points with close friends, family, and those with whom you work closely. These ideas may help others understand you better and teach them how best to interact with the lively Seven.

You want nothing more than to be appreciated for your incredible visions and inspiring new ideas! You are happiest when others are following you like the Pied Piper, listening raptly to your stories, taking your lead on what to do next, and engaging with you in laughter and upbeat conversations.

Your friends and family members can make you happy by providing attention, affection, presence, and the freedom to pursue whatever your heart desires, when it desires. You may become upset with them if they try to change you or your approach to life.

> It's important that they love you just the way you are and give you the freedom you crave.

You expect others to take responsibility for themselves, and you will quickly sever connections with people who act needy or too clingy or anyone who tries to tell you what to do. Freedom is your middle name, and loved ones will do well to recognize and honour that about you!

You have lots of energy and optimism and want to make a contribution in the world. Your co-workers should know that despite your idealistic dreams, you can become overwhelmed by too many possibilities and end up paralysed and unable to take action.

You need instant gratification, and you place few (or no) limits on yourself in this regard. Friends will want to avoid judging your behaviour and choices, despite their inability to understand your appetites and lack of discipline.

One of the most challenging things your friends and co-workers will have to face in dealing with you is this very inability to restrict or limit yourself. Your only form of self-control comes from external sources (other people enforcing limits upon you), and you strongly resent it at the same time that you desperately need it.

As the happy-go-lucky Seven, you can also respond quite differently when you become frustrated. You may lash out in a rage that others find unexpected and off-putting. Friends are not likely to forget the intensity and depth of your anger!

Admirable Qualities of a Seven

As the eternally optimistic Seven, you don't let life get you down. You are the spontaneous, fun-loving, free-spirited lover of life. You find a way to appreciate all aspects of life, and you can make the most humdrum activity feel new and exciting. You enjoy being outspoken and having others listen to what you have to say.

> Part of the delight you take in life is shocking people with your outrageous behaviour and stories!

Your generous nature has you looking for ways to help others and trying to make the world a little bit better for you having been in it. You can't stand to see others suffering or sad, and you take it upon yourself to share some light-heartedness and laughter with them.

Being extroverted and friendly, you find it scintillating to meet interesting people, delve into new cultures, try novel experiences, and come up with imaginative ideas. Your interests are broad and varied, and you know a little about a lot of things.

You aren't afraid to take risks, speak out, or suggest an untried approach. Despite your playful nature, you have a very practical mind and can focus your skills and energies on worthwhile objectives.

Pressures and Limitations

Because of your many interests, it can be a challenge to find enough time to pursue all the avenues you'd like. You may find that you aren't able to finish projects because your attention is now focused elsewhere or you have moved on to the next greatest thing.

Having a wide breadth of interests and talents is great, but it can also be a negative when it keeps you from specializing or delving deeply into any one area. You miss out on the expertise that comes from committing to one particular industry or career.

The flighty Seven has a tendency to lift off and be ungrounded, getting lost in dreams, visions, and fantasies. You certainly don't like being stuck with the same thing every day. As as you might imagine, you can feel restricted and confined by long-term, monogamous relationships.

If you aren't judicious in where you apply your talents and energy, you can become scattered, undisciplined, and overwhelmed. Your constant need for new stimulating experiences can leave you feeling unfocused, impatient, impulsive, and totally exhausted.

You place a lot of pressure on yourself to keep up the never-ending stream of newer, bigger, and better experiences in an effort to stay happy and engaged in life. But feeling excited and intrigued all the time can leave you little room for feeling emotions, delving into the depths of yourself, or catching up on sleep.

As Children

You may recall being busy, busy, busy. You were an active child who sought out adventure and action! You were the one to marshal the neighbourhood kids and drum up some exciting new game or exploration.

You preferred playing with other children to playing alone without an audience. And you had a certain skill in managing the adults in your life; you could get what you wanted on a regular basis simply by wielding your charm where needed.

> As a child, you dreamt of the incredible feeling of freedom you would have when you grew up and became an adult.

It's possible that you experienced some type of childhood deprivation that kept you from having or experiencing all the things you felt you should. This clearly imprinted on you and explains your adult need for tasting everything that life has to offer.

It is highly likely that you were deprived of some basic nurturing as a child; as an adult, you seek what you need to ensure that you never go without again.

As Parents

Sevens tend to be enthusiastic parents who want their children to be exposed to as many different experiences and adventures in life as possible. You will generously and enthusiastically sign your children up for many enriching activities. Be careful not to overdo it—or you'll introduce your children to the feeling of being overwhelmed at an early age.

You so love being busy that you may find you are too engrossed in your own activities to pay enough attention to your children. Involving your children in your activities (when appropriate) can be a good compromise to this dilemma.

Tips for Living with Sevens

In Love

Your ideal partner adores you and enjoys participating in your many antics and adventures. He or she allows you to take the lead and will follow your whims and fancies, enjoys a high level of stimulation, energy, and variety, and doesn't need to dwell on the negative aspects of life (because you won't).

> The biggest challenge someone will have in a relationship with you is getting you to see that there is a problem!

You would rather keep your Pollyanna views of life than face the facts and deal with reality. Your ideal mate is someone who can charm and soften any upset, defuse any conflict, and sweeten any experience for you.

You will require your partner to reflect back to you your own high self-image and lofty perceptions of yourself. And when they do, you will shine! As the effervescent Seven, you are quite pleasant to be around when you feel admired and appreciated for who you are.

On the other hand, if your mate ever puts you down, makes fun of you, or challenges you, you will be quick to discount his or her opinions and ridicule his or her ideas. If your flow in life gets disrupted, you can be quite perturbed and upset. You perceive it as someone of a lesser mind bringing you down from your high in life, which makes you quite angry.

You are highly sensitive to the boring rut of relationships. You must have new activities, novel interests, and charming experiences in your daily life if you expect to have any spark in your relationship. At the same time, easy-going Sevens enjoy being in the flow of things.

You see people come and go in your life with ease and grace, and you enjoy ending connections on a high note—much like a performer leaving the stage after a successful joke. You may return to the connection again—but only if the flow reunites you with that person.

For the rambling Seven, commitments feel restrictive. Although you are capable of being in a committed relationship for a long time, you are still uncomfortable with the whole idea. You choose to see it as an adventure in order to make it palatable for you.

Your mate will love the support and encouragement you provide. Since you have so many varied interests, you will encourage your partner to explore whatever appeals to him or her. And you have the innate ability to appreciate the many facets of your beloved.

> You'll enjoy doing whatever your mate likes together—as long as it's varied and not monotonous.

In the Workplace

You are the great equalizer in the office, and you provide a wonderful, refreshing alternative to authority. Perhaps you suggest a true democracy or a group-vote approach; whatever it is, you can be sure it will be arranged so that no one is in charge and everyone can do what they like!

Your idealist ways of thinking and dreaming are wonderful, but you can become too insistent about ideas that are really not practical or efficient. You can also get lost in the theory and never get around to actually executing the idea. And if things become routine, you will be the first one to open up the floor to consider novel approaches.

Confrontation is not something you endure well; you'll sidestep the issues and go around the rules by redefining the facts or expanding the definition of the terms. You are very creative when it comes to getting your way!

In this same vein, you are skilled at altering people's minds to gain support for your pet project or idea, at rewording objections so they don't sound so objectionable, at inflating the possibilities so your idea sounds better than it is, and at proffering solutions that have no tactical details fleshed out. By using overarching generalities and ignoring all the holes in your theories, you frequently offer thoughts that sound like you're promising something (when you're really just postulating).

> Despite these shortcomings, you win the popularity contest at work! Everyone loves you.

You are a true pleasure to be around, and you bring liveliness and fun to the office. You have an intensely creative mind and are quite forgiving of others' shortcomings.

With open-ended projects, you are a star! And you'll find ingenious ways to align the work with your areas of interest so you can stay engaged and intrigued. You are an excellent networker, developer of plans, synthesizer of ideas and concepts, and creator of unique approaches.

You have a strong sense of your own self-worth and abilities, and you may find yourself comparing how you stack up against others as a way to feel alive and vital. Be careful that your positive self-assessment is not shattered by negative feedback.

You see the bright side of things and take pleasure in your ability to create and make things happen—even if you don't stick around long enough to see the final execution! Unfortunately, your easy optimism can also blind you to facing the cold, hard facts about a situation. It is important for you to work in a team environment with other fact-focused personality types to balance you.

Since you can grow bored easily at work, it is important for your employer to recognize this and to keep you involved in working on the latest and greatest ideas. You can help yourself by finding ways to make the routine more exciting to you. You may be the office social coordinator, instigating dress-down, wear-a-Hawaiian-shirt-to-work days and suggesting after-work gatherings at your pool.

You're not one to delve too deeply into issues or problems; you prefer to leave that for others. You prefer the scheming, dreaming, and planning—and the concepts and intellectual visions—to the everyday details of implementation.

Self-Preservation Measures

As the optimistic Seven, you tend to avoid unpleasant situations and feelings, including worry and fear. You enjoy spending time with your family and friends—people who love you and accept you the way you are. Having a home base is important to you since it grounds your values and interests and offers you a supportive community.

> You may feel that it's your job to entertain the troops at family gatherings;
> in your mind, the more the merrier!

You find many ways to enjoy life. You have actual adventurous experiences—and then you have the many times of retelling it and regaling others with your antics. To you, the retelling to an avid audience is just as much fun as the actual event was!

You are the spontaneous Seven, always up for a new thrill. The only reason you plan ahead is so you'll have a loyal entourage trailing behind you to admire your spirit and devil-may-care attitude. You surround yourself with positive people; all others are swept away by the flow of life.

Although you are a risk-taker, you use common sense and take measured risks. And despite the image you create that you are always off on an adventure, the truth is that you enjoy spending time around your home base, puttering around the house, and spending time with close friends and family.

In Relationships

You enjoy the challenge of a new relationship and will seek out people who fascinate you or love adventure. Sometimes you are so friendly and affectionate, and so filled with the joy of life, that others may misinterpret your gestures as seductive or enticing (even when you didn't intend it). This can land you in a big mess!

For you, connections need to contain action. Sitting around and watching television just won't cut it. You like to push the edge of the envelope, stretch the boundaries, and sometimes even step on your loved one's toes just to get a reaction.

> As the aesthetic Seven, you are drawn to interesting, complex, fascinating, stunning, exciting, and unusual things and people.

You seek out the newest, wildest, weirdest, and coolest places, experiences, and ideas, and you hope to rally your mate and friends behind you as you set off to taste the many flavours of life.

In your closest relationships, if you become bored or find there isn't the same energy in the connection, you will either compensate by romanticizing the person in your mind or backing off if you feel cornered and stuck. If you focus on the discrepancy between the reality of the relationship and your notions of it, you may become sad and frustrated.

Should you find yourself with a partner who avoids new experiences, adventures, and exciting thrills, you will be very unhappy. Your focus in life is on savouring every moment, living each experience to the max, and feeling the fullest joy from it. As a result, you need to be with someone who is of like mind and who will follow you to the ends of the earth, laughing and delighting in the ride.

You define yourself and your value in your significant relationships by your ability to amuse, entertain, and see the silver lining. Your self-definition is as the happy-go-lucky soul who sees life as eternally great and as one big playground. And while this is great for superficial interchanges with people, it can get in the way of deep intimacy in your closest love connection.

You avoid feeling your feelings (at least any that you deem as negative) and do not willingly discuss pain, fear, loss, or anything else that might bring you down. This can become a wall between you and your partner.

Very few mates will want to stay blocked off from your deepest nature for long.

You can have a more fulfilling and intimate connection with your beloved if you allow yourself to gently explore the full gamut of your emotions, including the darker side of your nature. By touching into your suffering and pain, you develop a deeper bond with others; by sharing your feelings with your partner, you develop a more enriching, enduring relationship.

Socially

You are the eternal idealist and can imagine altering the course of your life to support the causes and groups you believe in. And although you can imagine this, the reality is that you are sometimes slow to take action on these motivations and good intentions, particularly if it means sacrificing some of your beloved freedom.

While your love of adventure and fun drives you, you are disciplined enough to subdue those desires sufficiently so that you can take care of your family obligations, career responsibilities, and charity work. Despite your commitment to do this, you resent the burden that all these aspects of your life place upon you.

> You seek fraternity and companionship—but only on your terms.

If others try to direct activities or control your behaviour, you want nothing to do with them. Your impatient nature drives you to take immediate action, even if you haven't thought it all through yet. Waiting around while others plan things out or figure out the details feels like having your teeth pulled.

Since you believe in the equality of all people, your sensitivities feel assaulted when you come across situations of inequality. In your nirvana, there would be no hierarchies, statuses, or classes, no power differentials, no leadership roles, and no one to boss others around.

As an interested Seven, your eager mind loves keeping up with the latest news, nationally and locally. You are connected, networked, and in the loop. Your large circle of close friends helps you stay on top of what's happening and keeps you up to date on many topics and industries.

> Seven's worldview: In a world brimming with opportunities and possibilities,
> I anticipate my next adventure.

Core Issues for Sevens

You fall into the trap of believing that you can avoid suffering and pain, avoid negative emotions, and avoid fear by keeping your life upbeat, happy, and idealized. You'll go to extensive lengths to keep from feeling frustrated, constrained, limited, restricted, boxed in, cornered, or enveloped by pain.

Somewhere along the way, you lost sight of the fact that life is a complete spectrum of good and bad, positive and negative. You came to believe that in order to live a happy life, you had to be free of limits, negative feelings, and negative people and experiences. And then you took it to the extreme, chasing after an overabundance of the highs in life in an attempt to keep yourself up all the time.

By trying to avoid pain, you create pain; striving to only experience the highs and positives of life limits your full expression and the experience of your humanity. When you recognize that you are actually an escapist who is running away from half of life, you begin to accept the fullness of life—the joys, sorrows, happiness, and pain.

This means welcoming life as it is in the moment—not as you wish it was or dream it could be. So if you're bored, embrace your boredom and sit in the quiet. In order to do this, you'll need to tone down the excesses, learn to delay your gratification, and only experience what is here and now and readily available.

As you do this, you'll begin to develop more compassion and empathy for others and the range of feelings they experience. You'll also begin to care more about their well-being and state of mind, even when it's not positive.

It will take some concerted effort on your part to rein in your externally focused energy and future-oriented dreaming and to focus your thoughts and energies on the present moment. Once you learn to go deeply into your current state of being, to feel your present emotions, and to be okay with whatever is, you will be on the road to expressing and living from your whole self.

Sample Questions

- When was I dreaming of the future and not focused on the present moment?
- What caught my attention and drew me into the realm of possibilities?
- Where has my energy been directed lately—into future adventures or into the here and now?
- Have I tended to overlook others' feelings and focus only on my wants?
- How did I respond to obstacles that got in my path?
- How have I reacted to negative situations and feelings lately?

The Core of Healing

- Begin to see how you are limiting yourself by seeking only the ups and highs in life.
- Be willing to make and keep commitments.
- Pull your energy and attention into the present moment and accept it the way it is.
- Start noticing how others feel and what is going on with them. Develop compassion.
- Accept and open up to uncomfortable feelings like sadness, pain, and suffering. Walk through them instead of batting them away like pesky gnats.

Affirming Change

Affirmations, when used properly, are powerful tools for change. Affirmations are designed to speak directly to the subconscious mind and effect change on a level much deeper than your rational or conscious thoughts.

To use affirmations effectively, it's important to feel what you're saying and accept it as valid and real. Therefore, it's helpful to begin with an affirmation that allows you to release old beliefs and any thoughts that are no longer serving you. This is followed by a positive affirmation that brings in a new idea.

Begin by saying both affirmations. Once you feel comfortable saying the second affirmation, you can drop the first one and just use the second one:

- I release my need to overextend myself by always feeling that I need to do and be more. I let go of the belief that external things will make me happy.
- I now choose to live more in the present moment, recognizing that I am happiest when I am calm and centred. I know that there is enough for us all, and I am profoundly happy and grateful to be alive.

Opportunities for Growth

Watch yourself and notice when you are being drawn to novel experiences and possibilities. By becoming aware of the allure of stimulating opportunities, you can short-circuit your response. Remember that choosing continually heightened pleasures can be a way to avoid feeling your emotions.

Pay attention to other escape routes that you enjoy, such as taking on too many projects simultaneously, continually scanning the horizon for the next big thing, spending too much time dreaming about your visions for the future, and any other creative mental evasion techniques you favour.

Recognize that by shifting your focus to something fun and exciting instead of taking concrete action now, you are simply procrastinating and avoiding committing to completing your current project. Call it what it is! In addition, when you spend all your time in superficial pursuits, you effectively avoid any kind of deep experiences or substantial reflections about yourself.

> Monitor your tendency for gluttony.

After all, gluttony combined with feelings of entitlement leads you to believe that you deserve only the best in life. And when you feel your self-worth being questioned, be aware of the fear that comes up for you. Feeling inferior to others is not a comfortable feeling for you!

When you receive constructive feedback about yourself or your behaviour, be aware of your tendency to interpret any type of evaluation as pejorative or critical. Open up to the possibility that there might be a kernel of truth for you in the comments being made.

Experience the feelings that come up for you—and dig through the feedback to find what morsel you can glean from the comments. Allow the feedback to sink in in the manner in which it was intended—and stop trying to disarm the situation with your abundant charm and humour.

When life's possibilities dance before your eyes, be willing to turn away from them and commit to your current course of action or project. Challenge yourself to accept the full scope of commitments and responsibilities that you have taken on in life—and do so without umbrage or resentment.

Become an observer of yourself, watch for your impulsiveness to arise, and start a new habit of simply observing the impulse instead of taking action on it. As you watch the impulse, eventually it will pass. In time, you'll get better at assessing which impulses are worthy of action and which should just be allowed to pass by. Doing so will help you focus on helpful things and on areas where you can grow. You'll find that you have less furtive mental states once the stimulation level has been dialled down a bit. Learn to ground yourself in the present moment and accept what is.

Start really listening to friends and family members and comprehending their feelings (both good and bad). You will learn many new things about them and may begin to appreciate that your well-being is intrinsically connected to theirs. Find an appreciation for quiet and solitude.

> It's not necessary or wise to distract yourself 24/7.

If you feel anxiety arising, sit with it. Become friends with it. By learning who you are and what you are feeling, and by reducing the external stimulation in your world, you will come to a place of trusting yourself. And you may be surprised at how happy that makes you!

Understand that some things are better if you wait for them. Curtail your tendency to satisfy every whim on a moment's notice. Most good things are still available tomorrow or the next day, and that will give you time to discern what choice is best for you.

When it comes to having fulfilling, adventurous experiences, focus on quality rather than quantity. You can enjoy every experience more fully once you learn to bring your focus and attention into the present moment. When you enjoy what is happening right now and are not envisioning a future escapade, you will actually experience life (rather than missing it while you're off in a dream world).

Be certain that what you go after is what is really good for you. Consider the long-term ramifications of getting what you want because it may become a source of unhappiness if not chosen wisely. Your best bet for being happy is to find satisfaction in the moment … whatever it is.

Stages of Evolution

For every personality type, there are opportunities to live from several different stages of growth, depending on whether you are reflective and interested in growing or are happy with the status quo. In addition, not everyone who is a Seven will have every trait or quality described here. Some will have traces of a characteristic, and others will see that same characteristic in abundance. A general overview of each stage is followed by a more detailed description.

Deteriorating

Flighty, anxious, superficial, hyperactive, excessive, escapist, materialistic, unwilling to feel emotions, look for next big thing, feel deprived, live for tomorrow, feel empty, scattered, frustrated, feel trapped and restricted, impatient, irritable, critical, insensitive, harsh, impersonal, angry, venting, sarcastic, insecure, greedy, selfish, insatiable, out of control, panicked, terrified, erratic mood swings, compulsive, manic

When you feel deprived by life, you feel as though you are being unfairly restricted from having fun and experiencing enjoyable sensations, and you will seek out even more escapades. Unfortunately, in this state, you won't necessarily enjoy the experiences because you are in a compulsive mode, searching for more highs. Having so many experiences and not getting the same highs from them will leave you feeling empty and deprived, and the cycle will continue.

As you fall down the rabbit hole, you become even more restless, distracted, scattered, and unfocused. You race from one great idea to the next, never actually accomplishing anything. As a result, you become frustrated and try to create more organization and focus in your life. You decide that more self-control will help get you out of this pickle.

But even self-control is too controlling for you! You feel constricted and managed and like you can't breathe. Then you become even more frustrated, impatient, and angry. You may start to tear apart your own ideas before you even try to develop them. And you are unable to stop feeling deep disappointment with friends and life in general.

> Nothing satisfies you, fulfils you; or meets your expectations anymore.

You feel rigid, harsh, and overly critical with yourself and everyone else—until you have no more energy. You are completely spent, shot, done. You might become panicked or claustrophobic (which is symbolic of how you are feeling boxed in by life).

At your worst, you give up on yourself and life, retreat into deep despair and depression, become self-destructive, indulge in overmedicating, or attempt suicide.

Status Quo

Afraid to delve into the depths, seek immediate gratification, short attention span, adventure-seeking, spontaneous, burdened by responsibility, disappointed, restless, nit-picking, impulsive, desperate, infantile, offensive, abusive, excessive, demanding, self-centred, never have enough, tell stories, flamboyant, performing, afraid of being bored, constantly moving, exhausted, over-extended

Your happy-go-lucky self has now become far too serious for your own liking. You may try to teach others, argue with them, critique their opinions and views, or become terse and abrupt, less personal, less charming, and impatient. You become more controlling and rigid.

At this point, you will start picking at people's shortcomings, being extremely sarcastic and biting, and venting your irritation by yelling or reprimanding others.

> You are still following your impulses, but your impulses are now quite negative.

You may grow tired of being the performer and always being on for people; as a result, you withdraw from everyone, even your closest friends and partner. You seek isolation, privacy, and the opportunity to be left alone. Others will be caught off-guard by this uncharacteristic behaviour!

No longer able to discern what you really want, you feel hyperactive and unable to say no to yourself, unable to deny yourself anything. You do or say whatever pops into your mind without editing or restricting yourself or thinking about the impact on others. Your behaviour may become flamboyant, exaggerated, overdone, or overly dramatic.

You grow resentful of having to marshal everyone for fun, become preoccupied with yourself and your interests, and are almost obsessively single-minded. Your energy and body language will tell others to leave you alone, and you'll make no effort to entertain or amuse others. All of this is an attempt to restore yourself, re-energize, and recover.

The Alarm

When you become aware that you are always seeking the next best thing and that it is always just around the next corner, you can begin to alter your experience of life. Once you have this awareness, the next step is to learn to *be* in the moment, to enjoy the experience while it's happening (not in the anticipation of it or the retelling of it to an audience). And when you are able to be fully present in each moment of your life, revelling in it, celebrating it, and feeling it, you will know the true happiness that comes from living your best life.

Evolving

Desire more options, seek opportunities, adventurous, easily distracted, epicurean, sophisticated, up-to-date, knowledgeable, uninhibited, witty, entertaining, overcommitted, connoisseur, optimistic, rationalizing, idealistic, creative, fun-loving, happy-go-lucky, playful, high-spirited, practical, productive, prolific, accomplished, multi-talented, amusing, futuristic, planning, experiential

You are learning to appreciate and enjoy experiences as they occur and to explore the world and relish what you discover. You have reached a place of balance where you still pursue adventure, but you are also present and grateful for where you are now.

You are able to relax more and understand any feelings of discomfort that come up. You can be with your feelings instead of running quickly in another direction. Your mind is quieter, calmer, clearer, and more able to focus and concentrate; as a result, you are tapping into deeper insights and creative energy.

You have self-control and are able to prioritize without forcing yourself to be a certain way or restricting your choices. Your real interests and creative urges guide you—instead of a frenzied desire to do more of anything. Since you are pursuing your real desires and dreams, you are much more productive and satisfied with life.

On Your Spiritual Path

Appreciative, grateful, happy, in touch with feelings, caring, compassionate, considerate, thoughtful, awed by beauty and simplicity, joyous, responsive, enthusiastic, invigorated by life, excitable, lively, resilient, cheerful, eager, inventive, life-loving, experience life freely, connect with people deeply, able to concentrate, versatile, delighted, extroverted, exuberant, excellent networker, fun, free, ecstatic, spiritually tuned in

Your ability to focused, concentrate, and integrate information without going off on tangents results in you being grounded, having real confidence in yourself and your abilities, and learning to trust your inner guidance.

> The world becomes a fascinating place in every moment—not just when you're on a crazy lark or a wild adventure.

You discover the depth and revelation of life no matter what you're doing or where you are. And boredom is no longer a concept you relate to; you've become the ultimate connoisseur of life's mysteries and essence.

Each experience feels meaningful and profound, leaving you deeply appreciative and intensely grateful. The simple things in life awe you: the beauty, the wonder, the joy, and ecstasy you stumble upon daily. You now live in the abundant universe where life provides plenty of bliss and goodness to you!

Type Seven: The Aficionado

Life is a bowl of cherries for you, and you make every effort to avoid experiencing any of the pits! You love to splash in the fun of life and delight in leading others on adventures and escapades. Later, you'll get just as much pleasure from regaling the details of the story to a rapt audience as you did in having the experience in the first place.

If it were up to you, you'd never have to face your feelings or deal with negative people, authorities, or power structures. However, continuing to live in your Pollyanna world will lead you down the proverbial rabbit hole into a dark abyss.

You find it challenging to impose any self-control or discipline on your impulsive nature, and you look to others to enforce the rules and boundaries that keep you in check. And when they do, you resent the limitations and restrictions they put on you.

You enjoy contributing to the world and bringing joy to others, but you don't feel the compassion and caring on a deep level that enables you to empathize and be present for another's pain.

> As a result, some people will love you and enjoy your antics, and others may perceive you as aloof or self-centred.

If your tendencies are allowed to grow unchecked, you will become obsessed with pleasure-seeking stimulation and will receive less gratification from the experiences. In order to grow and realize your full potential, you will need to recognize that life is a spectrum of all possibilities (positive, negative, and everything in between) and that you can't expect to ride the crest of the wave 24/7.

By learning to be present in the moment and enjoy what's in front of you (instead of always living for tomorrow), you will overcome your allergic reaction to being bored and will begin to appreciate life in all its forms and varieties. When you are able to comfortably be with your emotions (positive and negative), you will develop more empathy and compassion for others and deepen your connections and intimate relationships.

As you welcome life with its myriad shapes and configurations, you become a true connoisseur of experiences and people, and you begin living up to your fullest potential as the ultimate aficionado of life.

My greatest virtue is my strong sense of justice and unerring willingness to protect the underdog.

If you betray my trust, you can kiss our friendship good-bye.

I don't beat around the bush and I like taking charge.

I become restless and impatient with others' incompetence.

I'll show them who's really in charge.

I support, empower, and protect those close

Type Eight
The Competitor

At my best, I'm loyal, positive, honest, generous, and supportive.

I like being independent and self-reliant.

Watch what you say and do because I'll never forget it.

At my worst, I can be demanding, uncompromising, possessive, arrogant, and quick to find fault.

My deepest fear would be having to submit to someone.

8

Type Eight—The Competitor

As Type Eight (the Competitor), you come across directly, saying what you mean without beating around the bush. You are a natural born leader and aren't afraid to take charge. You enjoy being independent, making your own decisions, and charting your own path.

As the honest Eight, you are forthright, assertive, and resourceful. People perceive you as powerful, strong, magnanimous, and decisive. You enjoy protecting others who don't have as much on the ball as you do. And there isn't much in life that can scare you or cause you to back down.

> Your charisma and sheer presence draw people to you and make them want to follow you.

You convey confidence and have a take-charge approach to everything. You are proud of your ability to overcome anything and believe that adversity only makes you stronger.

Your imposing presence, ability to soak up the excitement of life, and desire to experience everything to the hilt cause people to marvel at you. You have never heard of too much of a good thing!

When you give your word, people can count on it; on the other hand, you are not tolerant of fools. You can be intimidating and too blunt at times, and others can misinterpret your manner as insensitive or thoughtless. You dominate a room with your larger-than-life presence and may be perceived as overly aggressive or cocky.

Your idea of being authentic is to say what you mean and mean what you say. You won't back down when others challenge your opinions or beliefs—even if they can prove you are wrong or when it's in your own best interest to do so.

Challenges are everyday fare to you, and you find them exhilarating and fun. Your ever-present sense of humour helps you see the light side of most situations, even the painful ones. In fact, although most will never know this, behind your armour coating is a sweet, playful nature.

An unusually devoted and protective mate and parent, you will do anything to take care of your family and provide for them, even if it means you secretively have to go without. You live by your own code and have a strong sense of right and wrong. Injustice compels you to action, and those you protect will be loyal to you.

It's important to feel self-reliant, in control of your feelings, and self-confident. Whether people like you is immaterial to you, but they do need to respect you and your authority. People must treat you fairly or risk offending your sense of justice; at times like that, they won't want to witness your strong, stubborn, forceful nature!

> You are the king of your castle, the master of your hearth, and the commander of your ship!

As long as everyone knows and honours your position, life with you will be easy. You will make sure everyone is provided for (in the way you decide is best, of course), and they will feel grateful and loyal in return. However, if your loved ones challenge you, question you, catch you off guard, hurt you, or expose you, watch out!

Being treated poorly or unjustly is one of your secret fears. You never want to appear vulnerable, soft, manipulated, or weak. Anyone who tries to impose his or her will upon you should be prepared for a strong onslaught in return. You will resist without analysing the validity of the suggestion or idea!

You also fear being deprived of what you perceive as the basics for your survival. You will go out of your way to stay strongly independent, not relying on anyone for anything, and will always ensure that your needs are met. Ironically, your basic needs are probably far nicer than most people's wants are. You dislike mediocrity and enjoy providing yourself with nice things.

In a Positive, Healthy State

As the decisive Eight, your need for self-reliance helps you grow strong, confident, capable, and adept. Your resilience and persistence are strong traits that leave you little compassion for others who allow caution or anxiety to slow them down.

> You enjoy being the centre of attention, the one who doles out advice, the expert, the know-it-all, the boss, the leader, and the go-to person.

You can get others to do exactly what you wish by using power and assertiveness, invoking the concept of justice, and simply directing people to do your bidding.

Your authoritative approach to pretty much every aspect of life puts you in the big dog category. You are the one to rally the troops, take charge, develop a plan, and command others. You are also a strong visionary with an eye for the big picture. Sometimes you disregard pesky details in order to implement a flashy solution that you dreamed up!

Action is what you like to focus on (not strategies). You love implementing powerful ideas that will blow people away! Retelling the story to an avid audience is half the fun of it—with you as the hero who saves the day.

You are clearly capable of differentiating between rational and irrational courses of action; however, you have no difficulty blurring the two when it suits your wishes and objectives. You have a strong, vivid imagination and find it frustrating when others don't follow concepts that you espouse, especially when they seem so clear and obvious to you.

> If there were a superhero personality type, you would be it!

Your greatest virtue is your strong sense of justice and your unerring willingness to protect the downtrodden, weak, and vulnerable in society. Your big heart and generous nature have you extending yourself to protect and help others, even at your own expense.

When you give your word, people know they can count on it. You call it like you see it, assess things quickly and accurately, and simplify complex problems. You cut to the truth of the matter in any situation and take decisive action (right or wrong). You are a natural born leader, and others love to follow you!

In a Detrimental, Unhealthy State

Your deepest fear is of having to submit to someone. When you are not feeling strong and self-confident, you can lash out at others or try to control them in an effort to protect and defend yourself. Paradoxically, this makes you even more dependent upon others and escalates your fear and panic.

When you are stressed, you believe that your way is the only way, your truth is the truth, your opinion is the right one, and your interpretation of justice is the only one. You perceive life as a battle of wills, have trouble backing down or admitting you're wrong, and can become confrontational, intense, or argumentative.

When you feel backed into a corner, you need to prove that you are the boss. You tend to push things too far, trample people in the process, act too abrasively, and become overly aggressive and unable to control yourself. Conflicts escalate when you overreact or become overbearing.

> The inability to self-regulate is one of your weaknesses.

You take things to extremes, indulge in excesses, and overdo things. When you desire something, you want more of it. To you, there is no such thing as too much.

When you perceive someone as your enemy, you will capitalize on any weaknesses to gain an advantage. Controlling others' behaviour is one of your tools (along with manipulative vengeance, wrath, guilt, and overpowering others).

You see people as weak or strong, dull or bright, dumb or smart. And when you assess another as inferior, you take advantage of your upper hand. In your immediate circle, your attitude is "my way or the highway," and you are more than willing to watch people leave if they won't follow your lead.

Your focus in on power—who has it, how much they have, and whether they are willing to use it. If there is a power vacuum, you will instinctively step in and fill it. Like the general assessing a wartime situation, you are unending in your quest for power, justice, truth, and the ability to influence others to do your will.

At your worst, you may ignore your physical needs by avoiding medical care and routine check-ups, indulging in overeating rich foods, or abusing tobacco and alcohol. You tend to push yourself far too hard and place undue stress on yourself, which can lead to strokes or heart problems. And while you generally want to feel in control, you are also prone to alcohol and narcotic addictions.

Tips for Getting Along with Eights

You might want to share some important points with close friends, family, and those with whom you work closely. These ideas may help others understand you better and teach them how best to interact with the proud Eight.

You enjoy coming to the point, being direct, and speaking your mind—and you expect others to do the same. You have a hard time understanding people who beat around the bush or don't say what they mean.

> You are highly confident and rely upon your abilities and skills.

You want people to stand up for themselves, and you expect friends and family to defend you and stand up for you. After all, you'd do the same for them! You can be very protective of others. You are not a gossip, and you won't tolerate others talking behind your back. If someone betrays your trust, they can say good-bye to your friendship. You're one of the most loyal and trustworthy types.

If others want to get your attention, they need to speak strongly and directly to you, telling you exactly what they want and what they need from you. And while you enjoy being acknowledged for your many contributions, you draw the line at gratuitous flattery. You'll have none of that!

Your assertive, bold nature is your natural style, but others can easily misinterpret that as an attack on them or feel as if you're yelling and angry. They will need to understand your ways in order to not take your manner personally.

You want people to be vulnerable and share their innermost feelings with you. You long for them to see your tenderness and soft interior. However, you also have a habit of screaming, cursing, and stomping your feet when you're irritated—and you want everyone to understand that that's just the way you are.

It's a challenging proposition for people to expose their vulnerable sides to you, only to see you ranting and raving a short time later. It doesn't feel safe to others.

> There are times when you need to be alone; you need your space.

Co-workers and loved ones will be wise to honour your need for space so that you can recharge your batteries.

Admirable Qualities of an Eight

Your independent streak is a mile wide, and you insist on being self-reliant and self-supporting. While you're happy to help others out, you prefer to take care of things for yourself. You're a natural take-charge kind of person and enjoy tackling tough challenges that others shy away from.

As the courageous Eight, you can be trusted to be honest and forthright—to tell it like it is. Helping, supporting, and empowering others makes you feel good. Your family will never know what it means to go without as long as you're around.

You are the protector of those who can't or won't protect themselves, and you are an asset to any cause you volunteer for. Charities love having you on their teams!

As the maverick Eight, you relish getting every last drop of enjoyment out of life. Taking things to the extreme and wanting the best of everything are part of your make-up. You are here to enjoy the ride of life!

Pressures and Limitations

You can come across like a ton of bricks sometimes! People may feel overwhelmed by your directness and shy away from you—even when you're not intentionally trying to scare them.

> To you, this is just speaking your truth, but others may consider it an assault at times.

Suffering fools and incompetent people is not something you do well. You grow quite impatient with people who don't do a good job, and you may feel restless and agitated if you have to work with them for long.

As much as you reach out to help others and protect people, it chafes you to not receive appreciation for your efforts. You are sticking your neck out for people, and they can't even thank you!

You have a long memory when it comes to slights, insults, and injustices—and you like to hold a grudge for a long time. You expect others to make it up to you eventually, or you'll just keep on carrying the scorecard around.

You are very hard on yourself and put way too much pressure on yourself. And because you are good at making and following your rules, you get irritated when others don't follow the rules or when things don't go the way you planned. How dare life not comply with your agenda!

As Children

You may recall being a very independent child; you had a strong inner spirit and a feisty attitude. You may have spent a lot of time alone, enjoying solitude over the company of other children.

> As the intimidating Eight, you want to take control of situations and don't like anyone controlling you.

You were known to assault other children verbally or physically if they bothered or provoked you. And you would watch people (children and adults) to determine their weaknesses so that you could use that knowledge at some future date.

You perceived yourself as the strongest, fittest, most powerful person in your family; as a result, you would take charge of things that most children didn't get involved with. You may have grown up in an abusive or challenging home that taught you to be tough and not take anything from anybody.

As Parents

Eights tend to be loyal, devoted parents who are very caring and like to be actively involved in their children's activities and lives.

At times, you may be overly protective of your kids, and you are known for your unyielding, demanding, bossy, controlling attitude towards your family. You dictate how it will be, and you fully expect your children to do it your way—no questions asked.

Tips for Living with Eights

In Love

You're a lively one in your relationship, and you seek out a partner who is as independent and strong as you are. Your idea of intimacy and connection is lively arguments, romping sex, and fun adventures.

> Your sexuality brings you great joy, and you will match your mate's enthusiasm and intensity in this arena.

Your love of excess in all forms means you stay up late, enjoy partying and entertaining, and tend to binge on your favourite foods and drinks. Too much of everything is just about right for you! Your motto could be: *Why stop when you can always have more? There's never too much of a good thing.*

You are all or nothing—either all work and no play or all play and no work. You haven't learned how to live in the middle ground. As a result, your partner may feel overwhelmed by trying to keep the various parts of your life in balance.

You enjoy making the rules and making everyone in the house follow them. But once in a while, you grow bored with your own rules—and you'll break them (but no one else can unless you authorize it). This is just a way for you to amuse and entertain yourself, but it creates a crazy feeling in your home if family members can't follow what's going on and don't know how to please you.

You will go through periods of strict behaviours (like diet or exercise routines) followed by periods of total disregard for your own habits (binge eating, indulging too much). It's a challenge for your loved ones to keep up with your volatile, episodic way of living.

This desire for total control over your home territory (and your office if you're the boss) comes from your deep-seated fear of being controlled. You would rather die than have someone else control you!

You attempt to control everything in your environment, including your family's schedules, personal belongings, beliefs, physical spaces, hobbies, friends, eating habits, and intentions.

> You think you know your loved ones better than they know themselves.

You will determine the intentions behind their actions—and you will insist that those are their intentions even if they vehemently deny it. You don't trust them to know their own minds. In a close love relationship, this can be problematic. You won't trust your partner's motives and will assign motives to him or her (based on your fears). Your partner won't feel seen or acknowledged because you're always trying to tell them what to think (instead of listening to what he or she really thinks).

You need to be on top of all information relating to your partner and family. You don't do well with ambiguity and want clear-cut, concise answers to your many drilling questions. You may interpret your partner's minor oversights as a betrayal of your trust; you believe that they overlooked something critical or didn't consult with you before making a decision (even a minor one). These infractions will cause you to doubt your partner's trustworthiness.

If emotions come up for you, you quickly escape from your feelings by withdrawing and feigning boredom with the conversation. You may look back at all the times you did the same thing and berate yourself for your failures.

Despite your desire for people to recognize your soft underbelly, you really don't allow others to hurt you in any way. If your loved one does manage to upset you, you will not become vulnerable and willing to explore your feelings. You will immediately start manipulating the situation and the facts around what happened in an attempt to place the blame at your partner's feet. And in many cases, you'll begin plotting your revenge for how you'll make them wish they'd never hurt you.

When times are tough, you are a rock. You are the supportive, encouraging cheerleader who will strongly buoy your partner until he or she gets through the rough patch.

> You rise to the occasion when things are challenging, and you are a wonderful, stable, positive influence.

In the Workplace

The minute you step into an environment, particularly a work situation, you assess who is in charge. You address that person in an effort to establish and assess his or her worthiness to hold the leadership position. If you find the person worthy of leading, you will consider him or her an honoured opponent or you will respect the position.

You always keep your eye on anyone who is a strong candidate to lead a project, control a situation, or command the loyalty of others. And you are concerned about which side your subordinates are on—your side or the other side. In your mind, there is no grey area; they are either for you or against you, and you want to know which it is.

You demand a clear answer about who has your back and who doesn't. Unfortunately, your polarizing behaviour causes two factions to form, provoked by your grilling and insistent questions.

In the office, you control the hierarchy and are typically the boss. You enjoy controlling the work environment by defining rules and limits, and you ensure that everyone is treated fairly. But you are not one for compromising because you see it as a sign of weakness.

Your concern for justice and fairness is pervasive. You feel strongly that people should be protected, but you also encourage them to learn how to stand on their own two feet.

And while you love to enforce your rules, you allow yourself to break them when it's to your own advantage. Your agenda created the rules; in your mind, there is no conflict. To others, it appears confusing and hard to follow. *Does he want us to follow the rules or bend the rules?*

> Everyone who works with you will know that your motto is "My way or the highway," and you quickly show anyone who won't abide by it to the door.

When you are angry, you are forceful and direct. You tell other people exactly what you're upset about and don't carry hidden agendas. Once you've vented, you aren't likely to carry a grudge at work.

One of your foibles is that you demand to be kept informed about every detail. And if someone fails to tell you something (even innocently), you assume that they are trying to manipulate you or fool you in some way. You are concerned about any piece of information that you learn about after the fact, and you'll make a big deal about it to ensure that it doesn't happen again.

Self-Preservation Measures

As the powerful Eight, you know how to express yourself, especially when you are angry and feel as though something is unjust. You are very good at providing for your needs and never go without plenty of comfort, food, drinks, or emergency extras.

Should the necessities of your life (as you define them) not be in place, or the details of your life not be in order, you will feel off-balance and out of sorts. Having access to resources is vital to your well-being.

And you want to provide for yourself! Being able to feel independent and take care of your own needs is important to you. You want to support yourself and your loved ones financially—and in all ways. You are not one to go to others for money or help.

> And once something belongs to you, whether it's a possession or a person, you will protect it and keep it safe.

In general, you like to feel safe and will choose a seat where you can survey what's happening, see the door, see who's coming and going, etc. If someone sneaks up on you or surprises you, you are not amused. Being in control of your environment is tantamount to you feeling safe in the world.

In Relationships

As the assertive Eight, you can be too strong and direct for some people's liking. As a result of your brash personality, you enjoy associating with high-energy people with intense personalities. Those who have flat, dead energy are of no interest to you.

There is a fine line between your need to possess and your desire to surrender to your partner. While you enjoy showing your loved one your soft, sweet underbelly (once you trust them), you will never fully let go of your need to control them. In fact, you aren't sure whether you really want a mate who you can take care of or a mate who will stand up to you!

And, boy, do you love a good fight! In fact, you feel intensely close to your partner when you are fighting. You love how it evokes the truth of any situation. On the other hand, if you are constantly bickering with your mate, you will grow weary of the relationship. You love to pick a fight, but you don't particularly like it when your mate starts one. It's all about having control of the relationship.

You are drawn to people who are direct, independent (with the show promise of being someone you can control), and aren't afraid to argue for certain beliefs or points of view.

You are looking for a good lover and sparring partner—all rolled into one!

Your mate should know that he or she will always want to discuss things with you before taking any actions or making any decisions. If he or she doesn't, no matter how small or trivial the matter is, you will interpret it as betrayal, manipulation, or withholding something.

If a matter involves you, then you must be consulted because you believe anything to do with your partner or your family is in the realm of what affects you. After all, you feel the need to control and manage every aspect of your family's life.

Your partner will be wise to divulge every feeling and thought to you because you become irritated quickly when you discover that someone has held back and not shared everything. You may accuse your partner of not telling you his or her feelings—even when he or she isn't even sure about those feelings yet. In your all-knowing view of life, you think you know your partner's true feelings—and you want your mate to admit what is going on with them. As long as the person defers to your wisdom, all is well. But if he or she disagrees with you (even in describing personal feelings), you will not take it well.

You are quite leery of anyone you perceive as trying to get in the
way of your relationship.

You worry that someone is trying to come between you and your beloved, that someone will take him or her away from you, or threaten your relationship. As a result, you may try to isolate your partner from people you perceive to be threats. In your world, anyone you can't control is a potential threat!

Socially

You have a tough time trusting people and won't let your guard down until you're sure you know where they stand, where you stand, and whether they fully respect you. In fact, even once someone is considered a friend, you continue to test his or her loyalty to you. Once you have concluded that he or she is loyal, you are a friend for life and will have his or her back at every turn.

In fact, you frequently take up for your friends or those who have less power in a situation. You want them to learn to stand on their own and be self-reliant, but in the meantime, you are happy to protect them and ensure that they are treated fairly.

In a group setting, you will quickly figure out which people have the power (official or unofficial), and you will spend time getting to know them well. You feel a need to establish your authority with them and to feel that they respect you. In group settings, your natural tendency is to be the protector and make sure that justice is carried out.

You enjoy the scintillation of a debate or battle over justice or fairness and feel as if it brings out the best in you. You feel larger than life when you are struggling for the underdog's right to be treated equally.

And while you are typically loyal to the end, if people cross a boundary of yours or appear to betray your trust (by your definition, not theirs), you will excise them from your life as if they never existed. You are not one to forgive and try to work things out.

> Eight's worldview: I defend and protect the innocent in a world that is filled with inequality and injustice.

Core Issues for Eights

Your basic fear is of someone hurting you or controlling you. In an effort to keep that from occurring, you try to control everyone in your life, manage your environment, and keep an eagle eye on your friends to be certain that you can trust them. If you can control your life and your destiny, you believe you will feel safe and protected.

In an effort to do this, you feel the need to be completely self-reliant, to prove your power and strength, to resist ever showing your soft side (other than to a trusted partner or your child), to develop an aura of importance that impresses others, to completely dominate your immediate environment and the people in it, and to always be on top of any situation.

You come across as assertive, powerful, direct, abrasive, egotistical, and domineering. When things aren't going the way you think they should, you become confrontational, get in people's faces, and intimidate others in order to get your way. Your temper flares quite frequently and scares many away.

> Because of the dominant stance you take in life, you have a hard time being vulnerable.

Even with your loved one, you are only vulnerable when you feel strong enough to be. At the first sign of uncertainty, you quickly retreat to your default mode.

At your best, you learn to master yourself, control your own nature, understand how to trust others, and use your power and influence to help others. You lead worthwhile organizations and generously support needy groups. You can be the larger-than life hero—magnanimous, personable, charismatic, and inspiring.

In order to live as your best self, you will want to learn how to approach each situation in life with a fresh, open perspective—without trying to influence it to go your way. When you see the validity of other people's views and thoughts, you will be well on your way.

Sample Questions

- Did I just go after what I wanted without thinking about the possible implications or effects on others?
- How quickly did my temper come out?
- Did I simply assert my view or did I listen to hear if others had opinions?
- What is my impact on others—do they withdraw, resist, or stand up to me?
- How did I control that situation?
- In what ways did I avoid feeling my emotions and recognizing my concerns about being hurt?
- Did I remember to be considerate and soft towards my loved ones?
- What are my areas for improvement? What are my weaknesses?

The Core of Healing

- Learn how to rediscover your innocence and childlike nature.
- Recognize the appropriate amount of force or power that is being called for in each situation.
- Begin to modulate your response and become aware of your impact on others.
- Understand and appreciate the validity of others' truths.
- Allow yourself to trust, feel vulnerable, and experience your emotions.

Affirming Change

Affirmations, when used properly, are powerful tools for change. Affirmations are designed to speak directly to the subconscious mind and effect change on a level much deeper than your rational or conscious thoughts.

To use affirmations effectively, it's important to feel what you're saying and accept it as valid and real. Therefore, it's helpful to begin with an affirmation that allows you to release old beliefs and any thoughts that are no longer serving you. This is followed by a positive affirmation that brings in a new idea.

Begin by saying both affirmations. Once you feel comfortable saying the second affirmation, you can drop the first one and just use the second one:

- I now release any pent-up anger and any painful experiences from my mind and body. I release my fear of being controlled by others, my fear of loss, and my fear of being seen as vulnerable or weak.
- I now affirm that I am loving and loveable. I am worthy of respect and can be gentle without being afraid. I have a huge heart and let others share in the glory of the love I have to offer. My world is safe, beautiful, and peaceful.

Opportunities for Growth

As the bossy Eight, it is important to learn how to let others initiate things. Begin to relax, wait, watch, and listen before jumping in and directing. Pay attention to the valid logic of other people's opinions and behaviours and notice the consistency in their perspectives.

Recognize that your preoccupation with protecting, defending, controlling, and ensuring justice will cause people to either love you or hate you—and you'll end up with either a friend or an enemy as a result.

Practice directing and managing your anger so that it is doled out in appropriate amounts, at select times, and with the proper intensity. Whether you are denying, suppressing, or expressing your anger, they can all prove detrimental if you're not careful.

> When you find yourself wanting to stir up a confrontation, intensify a situation, or polarize a discussion, realize that this is a sign of your mounting insecurities.

Boredom can be a sign that you are unwilling to acknowledge your underlying feelings about people or situations.

Other techniques to mask your feelings are engaging in battles, challenging others to verbal duels, and indulging in excesses. Consider it progress to experience and feel your weaker emotions. It's important to know that you may initially feel depressed; this may be the window to your ability to be with your feelings. See it as a sign of forward movement, even though it may be uncomfortable in the short run.

As you begin to have insights about yourself, jot them down so you won't forget them or deny the issues. You have a gift for whitewashing and rewriting the truth of things; by recording your insights, you will be able to stay present with what is really happening.

> Come to a place of truly understanding that the world is not against you.

People in your life love you, respect you, and can be trusted (without being tested for years). Open up to the love and affection that is being offered to you. This won't weaken you; on the contrary, it will help you feel stronger, more supported, and buoyed.

It can be a vicious cycle when you choose to perceive the world as against you. When you come from this perspective, you resort to acting domineering, bossy, and obstinate. This behaviour will get a strong negative reaction from others who may take a hard stance or argue with you. And for others, your overbearing behaviour will only serve to alienate them.

Take an inventory of your friends and loved ones and really determine who is on your side and cheering for you. Then begin to let them know how important they are to you, express your feelings to them, and open up to those you trust.

This may feel challenging because forceful Eights don't want to be dependent on anyone other than themselves. However, without you realizing it, you are already dependent upon many people. The only difference is whether you admit it to yourself or not. Thinking you are entirely self-sufficient is simply a delusion.

Become aware of the overemphasis you place on power. You believe that power enables you to do whatever you want because you are feared and obeyed. But what you aren't getting is that those who respond like that to your powerful stature do not truly care about you as a person or love you for who you are.

> Understand that compromising doesn't mean giving in, retreating, or giving up.

Situations are not always win/lose or black/white. The world is not set up as a battleground where only the victor enjoys the spoils of life!

Change your perspective from the survival-of-the-fittest mentality to understanding that cooperative effort and partnership with others can help you accomplish more than you ever could by yourself when you were imposing your will upon everyone. In fact, when you come to the conclusion that real power involves being vulnerable at times and being open to others, you begin to know true intimacy and closeness in your relationships.

Once you experience a real connection in a relationship of equals, you know what it feels like to be loved, supported, and cared for. You will be able to yield to others at times and know that it doesn't mean you are inferior. You will find that you can let others lead the way without worrying about losing your power or influence.

You will learn to notice when you are feeling the need to dominate others—and will recognize that this is a signal that you are feeling uncertain and unsure. Rather than defaulting to the powerful feeling of domination, you can allow yourself to experience the underlying feelings—even if they seem scary at first.

And although it goes against everything you've learned so far, behave with self-restraint! That is when you exhibit true power and strength. You can live from your best self as an uplifter and inspirer of people. In a crisis, you are the one everyone wants to follow. Begin to show the depth of your feelings, your generous nature, and your huge heart.

> You'll be like the Pied Piper, and people will follow you anywhere.

Stages of Evolution

For every personality type, there are opportunities to live from several different stages of growth, depending on whether you are reflective and interested in growing or are happy with the status quo. In addition, not everyone who is an Eight will have every trait or quality described here. Some will have traces of a characteristic, and others will see that same characteristic in abundance. A general overview of each stage is followed by a more detailed description.

Deteriorating

Indulging in excesses, in-your-face, lustful, withdrawn, avoiding people, angry, short fuse, aggressive, explosive, confrontational, controlling, spiteful, destructive, addicted, feels mistreated, untrusting, suspicious, defiant, ruthless, dictatorial, renegade, con artist, immoral, potentially violent, delusional, invincible, megalomaniac, feels omnipotent, invulnerable, reckless, destructive, secretive, fearful, vengeful, barbaric, murderous, sociopathic tendencies

You haven't met a problem you couldn't tackle! You are assertive, bold, and aggressive in pushing to get your way, in grasping to gain control of the situation, and in always achieving your vision. Unfortunately, you leave wounded egos, emotional debris, and tattered relationships in your wake.

> People around you feel downtrodden, overlooked, beleaguered, and overwhelmed.

You are the creator of your own stress zone wherever you go. When you realize this, you may pull back, isolate yourself, or plan a strategy for retaking control. At times like this, you can become uncharacteristically quiet and secretive as you try to resolve the difficulties you see arising.

If you remain under stress like this for prolonged periods, you may become calculating, cynical, cold, or detached. Your soft side will retreat deep within you, and others will not know of its existence anymore.

You have a big problem with your temper; although you don't consider it an issue (*So what if I blow up once in a while? That's just who I am. Get used to it!*), others cower in the shadow of your tirades. Even when you're not angry, your presence is intimidating—even your gait is heavy and foreboding. When people hear you coming, they may feel anxious or nervous.

At your worst, your excessive indulgence may cause you to drink heavily, overeat, pick fights without cause, or become a workaholic or a sex addict.

Status Quo

Fear being deprived, fiercely independent, unwilling to compromise, angry, blunt, combative, intimidating, grandiose, impulsive, power-hungry, retaliatory, belligerent, adversarial, won't back down, threatening, demand obedience, instil fear in others, dominating, swaggering, forceful, my way or the highway, proud, egocentric, imposing, boastful, disrespectful, better than you, expansive, my word is law, insensitive, cynical, in denial about own emotions

Your ability to lead and guide others has gone too far, and you want to control everything in a misguided attempt to feel safe in the world. You don't know who to trust, and you may turn to those closest to you for reassurance that you are needed. (Notice that what you're seeking is to feel needed, not loved—this is an important distinction.)

187

Your sentimental side is evident to people with whom you feel safe and respected. To everyone else, you are a tough, independent, dominating person who is always in charge.

> In private, you may dote on your loved ones or pets—but only as long as they don't disappoint you or appear to betray you.

You need your loved ones to ask for your help and support—and to acknowledge their utmost dependence on you! In some cases, you will foster a complete and total dependence on you in an attempt to prevent them from abandoning you.

You will go out of your way to keep your loved ones from leaving or rejecting you, including using mind games, manipulation, emotional blackmail, lies, or undermining them to make them feel unbalanced and uncertain. Despite all of this, you are unwilling to recognize your own real needs or feelings, especially when someone you trusted has hurt you.

The Alarm

When you become aware of the internal feeling that you have to fight, push, and claw to make things happen in your life, you can come to a place of true surrender—a giving in to something greater and more powerful than you, something more lasting than your brief life. When you truly embrace this concept of surrender, you will be able to flow with life more easily, connect with others more deeply, and be your authentic self without fear of being rejected or hurt.

Evolving

Take charge, forthright, fight for justice, enforce fairness and equality, confident, protective, determined, enterprising, energetic, natural leader, quietly strong, generous, helpful, loved, connected, decisive, in control, fair-minded, dedicated, resourceful, clear, direct, interdependent, reliable, trustworthy, self-possessed, well-spoken, warrior for a cause, self-sufficient, pragmatic, wheeler-dealer, risk-taking, hard-working, financially independent, authoritative, take initiative, champion others, provider, honourable

When you realize that all human beings start out from a place of innocence, learn to truly trust others, and see their truths as valid, you become softer, more thoughtful, and caring.

> Your lust for life transitions into an intense passion for living fully and helping others.

You tap into your innate strengths of courage, fairness, intensity for life, and magnanimity. You feel safe in the world and start to open your heart and follow your generous impulses. You let down your guard and allow others to know you, the real you, not the trumped up façade you used to present.

As you do, you will discover how much you genuinely care about people and want to support them. You desire to be a force of good in the world and to share your bountiful love in healthy ways. You have figured out how to use your power and love simultaneously—and realize that those are not opposing goals.

On Your Spiritual Path

Make an impact on the world, receptive, open, honest, respectful, charming, inspiring, magnanimous, powerful, charismatic, interested in making and building things, want to make a difference, constructive, can-do attitude, courageous, joie d'vivre, in touch with feelings, open-hearted, caring, able to feel vulnerable, treat everyone equally, see other opinions as valid, considerate, heroic, in touch with a higher power, surrender need for control, sensitive, strong, passionate, merciful, have self-mastery, influential, truly great human being

You become aware of other people and their feelings—and are concerned about your impact on others. You have a magnanimous instinct and truly understand what it means to protect and serve.

> You are protecting people physically and caring for them emotionally.

You are in touch with your inner nature and have a calm, instinctual love for others. You are like a loving parent towards a child—except you are also able to see others as your equals.

You are like the barbarian who has conquered his kingdoms and won all the battles, only to wake up one day and recognize that it's not worth anything without love. Instead of overpowering others, you powerfully support them and protect them in a caring, nurturing way. You have come to the realization that feeling your soft, vulnerable emotions is a sign of strength, not weakness.

Others are drawn to you, inspired by you, charmed to be near you, and appreciative of your help.

> You have become the highest expression of your personality type—
> the powerful caregiver and protector.

Type Eight: The Competitor

Life is a battlefield, and you are the conqueror and ruler! Nothing is too much for you to take on or take control of. You are strong, forceful, dominating, and powerful. You impose your will on everyone and everything in an effort to have everyone do things your way.

You believe in sticking up for the little guy, the underdog, and those whom life has treated unfairly. Justice is your middle name. And although your intentions are honourable, your methods leave a lot to be desired! You leave devastation in your wake as you plough towards your goal at all costs.

Your personal truth is imposed upon anyone who will tolerate it, and you have no ability to value or honour others' truths. You know best, and you will make sure others understand that and appreciate your vision.

You may find personal relationships challenging as your loved ones grow and evolve until they decide they no longer want you to think for them. If you perceive their growth as a betrayal of your generosity and love, your personal life may be fraught with pain, which you will not acknowledge as having affected you.

If your behaviour deteriorates, you can become destructive, looking for revenge against people you perceive as having betrayed you or slighted you in some way. However, if you come to the conclusion that life is not a constant battle—and that you can simply let go and surrender to something greater than yourself—you can find and know peace and love. When you reach this place, life shifts tremendously for you!

> You become connected and caring, and you are able to express and receive love.

You see others as equals and value their opinions and ideas. You are ready to step into your highest potential and become the loving benefactor and protector (instead of the conquering barbarian). You come to the realization that the only worthwhile competition is the one with yourself—to see how much good you can do in the world before you die.

I like my ability to see different sides of an issue and be a good mediator.

I'll often bury myself in details, errands, and to-do lists rather than dealing with what I need to.

I have an uncanny natural ability to make people feel comfortable and good around me.

I love a good discussion, but I dislike confrontation.

I can overlook my own needs and desires, and I often repress my emotions, stifle my anger, and neglect my body.

I like to listen, help, and be of service.

Type Nine
The Mediator

Don't take advantage of my kind nature.

At my best, I'm generous, patient, and diplomatic. I like to keep the peace.

At my worst in a relationship, I can be unassertive, overly accommodating, passive-aggressive, and defensive.

I'm not into self-promotion.

I can be touchy about receiving criticism (warranted or unwarranted).

9

Type Nine—The Mediator

As Type Nine (the Mediator), you want nothing more than for everyone to get along and live in peace and harmony. You see yourself as laid-back, easy-going, unconditionally loving, and able to get along with almost anyone. Being agreeable, comfortable, calm, accepting, and approachable are important to you. In your ideal state, you would be content, humble, unassuming, and living free of any conflicts.

You have an uncanny natural ability to make people feel comfortable and good around you. They are at ease and can be themselves because you are so accepting of others, and you have a great talent for empathizing with others.

> You are gentle, considerate, and thoughtful. You go out of your way
> to ensure the well-being of others.

You are so helpful and in tune with others' needs that you can totally lose sight of your own needs and wishes!

As the reassuring Nine, you have an innate ability to see many diverse points of view, to notice and understand all the shades of grey in a situation, and to easily and calmly defuse tension and conflict in a crisis. You place more attention on the similarities between the parties than on the differences, and you make a fantastic mediator.

You are quite the intellectual, although you don't readily let people know this about you. You avoid conflict or being forced to react. You prefer to stay calm, steady, and peaceful. Sometimes this is to your own detriment since you can become so complacent that you minimize anything that upsets you.

Your downside is that you forget about yourself! You overlook your own needs and desires, repress your emotions, stifle your anger, and neglect your body. Sometimes this occurs because you have lost yourself in the simple beauty and pleasure of life, been swept up in the needs of others, or become overly focused on the mundane details of your life (errands, to-do lists, etc.).

When you allow yourself to be distracted like this, you fail to discover your own passion in life, what makes you tick, and what inspires you. As a result, you may never pursue your dreams.

You can become so caught up in the processes, procedures, habits, and routines of your life that you begin to move slowly, have a hard time making decisions, start procrastinating, and even have dull, heavy energy.

You also have a tendency to only share your opinions after everyone else does. This allows you to easily point out the errors in their ways of thinking. Your ability to successfully solve dilemmas is based on this process of elimination instead of an ability to logically deduct solutions.

> You are good-natured, happy, supportive, and open to others.

You want to unite with people and the world in order to feel harmony and group cohesion. You are receptive and patient, have great endurance and persistence, and are able to resist things that aren't right for you.

You enjoy being discovered rather than having to promote yourself; unfortunately, this doesn't happen very often since people tend to underestimate you as a result of your nonchalant, silent, peaceful, self-effacing manner.

You need to be appreciated and know that everyone around you is calm, relaxed, and happy. Otherwise, you can't relax. You also need your personal comforts and cannot go without them—things like your television time, your treats, your favourite foods, and your comfortable slippers.

You seek simplicity and harmony in life. Your strongly empathetic and intuitive nature has you so tuned in to what everyone is feeling that it's hard to feel at ease if there is unrest, chaos, or unhappiness in your immediate environment. Your home is your oasis, and you have set it up to nurture you and provide you with a safe respite from the world.

Since you fear being overlooked, ignored, left out, or shut down, you stay away from conflict and judgmental people.

> You worry that you won't find love, be loved, or experience giving love.

As long as you are unable to identify and meet your own needs, you will have a hard time in relationships. It's hard to have someone love you when they (and you) don't know who you are!

In a Positive, Healthy State

Your desire to find union means you usually open up to others and completely accept them as they are. People find this warm embrace from you a welcome change from the normal brusqueness of the world, and they will bond strongly with you.

You are a good talker and listener, and you will sit quietly instead of bringing up a dissenting point of view. You come across as reasonable, calm, responsible, thoughtful, mindful, and clear about the expectations of others.

You like to address things when you feel ready—and not a minute before—but you find it challenging to say no to people. In your world, yes means maybe, and maybe means no way. You think this is helping you avoid complications and conflict, but these unclear and misleading responses cause more problems than if you were more direct with your answers.

You have the strengths of acceptance, peacefulness, and being open and receptive. You easily relate to others and can recognize profound truths about life.

> At your best, you will be connected to both people and the universe.

You seek harmony in your world, are not afraid of hard work to demonstrate your love for something or someone, and are capable of making huge contributions to the world.

The steadfast, natural, down-to-earth Nine brings a sense of calm and peace to everything. You are patient, persistent, and willing to endure challenging circumstances in order to achieve a harmonious outcome.

Since you seek to identify and unite with others, you are a natural in a group setting. You provide a steady, reliable anchoring presence to the group and enjoy sensing and championing the needs and desires of whatever group you are a part of.

In a Detrimental, Unhealthy State

Your deepest fear is being separated from others, from life, and from the universe. You have a knack for deluding yourself about relationships—seeing connections where none exist, ignoring reality, or accommodating others to the point where you don't even know who you are or what's important to you.

From this state of illusion, you cannot realize a true, meaningful union. When you stop indulging in fantasies, accept other people, and give validity to your own needs, you will find a real connection and a loving relationship.

When you lose yourself in a situation or relationship, you feel a strong drop in your passion, excitement, and intensity. You may speak more slowly, use long, drawn-out sentences, have a heavily modulated tone to your voice, or give long, rambling explanations.

When you are at your worst, your desire to comfort yourself can be taken to extremes. You may overeat or under eat from your lack of connection to and awareness of your own body and emotions.

> The anger you have repressed all these years is eating you up.

You have a tendency to become slothful, lazy, and indolent, to avoid physical exercise, and to sit around far too much. You may turn to depressants, psychotropics, or excessive use of alcohol, marijuana, or narcotics in an effort to keep from feeling lonely and anxious.

These periods of inactivity can lead to forgetting about yourself and not meeting your basic needs or the needs of others in your life. You may become inattentive, forgetful, and commit sins of omission where you refuse to notice when someone needs your help.

As the conflict-avoiding Nine, most people think you are on their side because you haven't voiced your opinion or told them you're not. They don't know that you have a stubborn streak that you exercise through passivity instead of action. You are likely to hurt others by not doing what you said you would, not keeping your promises, or not following through. You use this passive-aggressive approach to make your voice heard—even though you won't speak up. You don't understand the implications of your passivity and inaction or how it can make you seem indifferent, cold, and callous to those you love.

You don't like feeling tense; in an effort to avoid it, you have developed several coping techniques (eating, getting lost in the details of daily life, and focusing on unimportant tasks and errands).

Sometimes your indecision and worry about hurting other people's feelings prevents you from taking necessary action.

> You need to recognize that by not making a decision, you are still making a decision.

Tips for Getting Along with Nines

You might want to share some important points with close friends, family, and those with whom you work closely. These ideas may help others understand you better and teach them how best to interact with the good-natured Nine.

How people ask you to do something is more important than *what* they're asking! You don't like it when people have expectations of you or try to pressure you into saying yes. You enjoy being of service and are a very good listener, but others need to be careful not to take advantage of your generous nature.

Although you tend to ramble and take the long way to get to the point, you want people to listen until you have finished speaking. You need time to spit it out and time to make decisions. Good friends are permitted to give you a gentle nudge or reminder (as long as it's done in a loving, non-judgmental way).

As the receptive Nine, you take in a lot of information and feelings from others. Sometimes you can feel overloaded by all the input; you need time to process everything. Friends and co-workers can assist you by asking questions that help you get clear on things.

Although you are self-effacing, you enjoy a good compliment as much as the next person does! Loved ones will want to remember to flatter you and tell you what you've said or done that they enjoyed.

> You are such an affectionate creature that it's only natural for you to
> want to receive affection in return!

Hugs, kisses, physical touches, and other gestures of love open you up to your deepest feelings. There's nothing you enjoy more than laughing with friends; it's one of the ways you splash around in life's bliss.

You are interested in good, invigorating discussions where everyone is treated respectfully and all opinions are valued. You are not, however, interested in confrontations or seeing people demoralized or put down. To you, personal opinions aren't important enough to warrant devaluing someone over theirs.

Admirable Qualities of a Nine

Accepting Nines do not judge others for their behaviours. You are caring and concerned about everyone you meet, and you have the ability to see many different facets of an issue, no matter how explosive it may feel to others. These skills make you an ideal mediator or facilitator in a group setting.

Most people love being around you! You are easy-going, fun, light-hearted, and welcoming. You enjoy knowing that people like your company, and you find it pleasurable to relax and have a good time with friends, old and new.

You have an innate gift of heightened awareness with regard to people's feelings, sensations, aesthetics, and the energy of any given space or moment. Despite being tuned into everything in your environment, you are able to easily go with the flow of life and feel connected and at one with life and the universe.

Pressures and Limitations

> Because you are so loving and peaceful, others sometimes judge or misunderstand you.

People may label you indecisive or too peaceful for their comfort level. As someone who is always sensing what others are feeling, you are touchy about receiving criticism (warranted or unwarranted); you may interpret every little raised eyebrow as a personal affront.

Your empathy for others can extend too far, causing you to care too much about what people think of you. You can be overly critical of yourself and upset about not having enough initiative or discipline.

Because you focus so much on others' feelings and needs, you are often confused about your own needs and desires ... and what you really want.

Your habit of speaking in long, drawn-out, rambling phrases and taking the long way around to get to your point results in people sometimes not listening to you or not taking you seriously.

As Children

You may recall feeling ignored and as if your feelings, opinions, desires, needs, and wants didn't matter. In order to cope with this, you tuned out a lot—especially when others were arguing or confrontational.

You tried hard to be a good child, and you suppressed or denied negative feelings, such as anger or irritation.

> You wanted to be around uplifting energies, but as a child, you had no control over who was in your environment.

As Parents

Nines tend to be supportive, warm, loving, and kind parents. You may be too indirect in your suggestions and guidance—and may be overly permissive at times—letting your kids get away with too much. But in general, your children feel loved and cared for.

Tips for Living with Nines

In Love

As a loving Nine, you bond for a long time and find it difficult to separate from a loved one, even if it's warranted. As a result, you may remain in a relationship for years after you should have left. You find it challenging to give up on the love you feel or let go of memories in order to make room for a new love.

When things aren't going well in a relationship, you place your attention on the nonessentials of life (errands, home repairs, etc.) rather than addressing and facing the real issues in your relationship.

> You may become withdrawn or uncommunicative and not have much
> to say to your partner.

You can retreat into your habits and the mundane details of life, finding lots to do even if none of it is necessary or important. This keeps you from engaging in the real relationship and facing the challenges. In most cases, the Nine's partner will be the one to have to spearhead change—if there is to be any.

When you become upset or frustrated, instead of dealing with the core issue, you may numb yourself through denial of the problem, escaping to a spiritual place of peace (i.e. excessive meditation), or attempting to live in a state of peace despite the signs to the contrary.

You, more than any other personality type, will try to run from life's paradoxes and tensions by transcending them or using simple solutions in a hasty attempt to patch things over.

Nines are so empathic and understanding that you have a habit of saying what people want to hear instead of what you are really thinking or feeling. Most of the time, you aren't even sure what you're feeling—and you spend all your energy tuning in to others. Because of this, your mate's needs will sound louder and feel more pressing than your own do.

You may fantasize about uniting with the ideal partner and being swept off your feet. You enjoy seeing your relationships as a merger of two people into one. As such, you tend to blame your mate when things go wrong and have a hard time seeing your role in the problem.

If you're not tuned in to your own needs and wants, you may forget yourself and focus solely on your partner's feelings and desires. This may feel idyllic to your mate for a time, but it will backfire in the long run. At some point, you will realize that you are not happy, and you will want to blame your partner for the situation. In order to avoid this potential quagmire, your loved one would be wise to help you recognize your needs and support you in meeting them,

As an optimistic Nine, you like it when your relationships flow smoothly, are stable, and lack conflicts.

> You enjoy having a peaceful, supportive, trusting, and accepting connection with your partner.

You wish that everything would solve itself! In most disagreements, you just go along with your loved one's wishes in order to keep a peaceful environment. You tend to simplify problems and minimize upsets; you may become inert, complacent, or stubborn.

The good news is that once you develop your own personal identity and know who you are and what you want, you will find that your intimate relationship can be even deeper and more connected because you no longer are at risk of losing yourself in it.

At your best, you are creative, optimistic, indomitable, and embracing; you are the glue that keeps the relationship together and heals old wounds. You create a harmonious environment and a loving home life, and you go out of your way to avoid creating any tension.

In the Workplace

Your ideal work environment is free of tension and friction; it is a place where everyone feels comfortable and gets along with minimal hassles and disagreements. You want to feel good—and have others feel good too.

When you receive positive support, praise, and recognition, you thrive and flourish! However, you aren't one to self-promote or ask others to notice you. In fact, you prefer when rewards, procedures, and hierarchies are defined clearly.

You are able to adapt to a predictable routine and dislike surprises and changes in how things are done. When you are on automatic pilot, you can produce massive quantities of work because you are an ideal employee who can forget about your personal agenda and put yourself 100 per cent into the job.

> Having positive, energetic, encouraging co-workers is important and keeps you productive and feeling good.

You tend to be cautious about making decisions and would prefer to go by the book and keep spontaneity to a minimum. You believe in doing what has worked before, avoiding taking too many risks, and minimizing the potential for disappointment. In some companies, this approach will be greatly appreciated; in others, it will be a poor fit.

When you are forced to make a decision, you will procrastinate by gathering information and attending to insignificant details instead of focusing on the decision. No matter how much you delay, you are known for coming through in the end with fantastic outputs or conclusions!

Having too much to do feels overwhelming, and you find it hard to focus on your priorities. You may fritter away the day doing a lot of nothing (which feels just as vital as the truly important things), but you are not eager to take guidance from co-workers or superiors.

When you are upset at work, initially you'll be quite passive in expressing your frustration by ignoring the situation, but later you will shift the blame to the organization's structure, procedures, management issues, or co-workers.

In general, you feel ambivalent about your superiors. You respect them, but you don't enjoy being told what to do. Even when you are having difficulty prioritizing your work, you are stubborn and don't want to listen to helpful input from your boss.

Self-Preservation Measures

> You enjoy comforting yourself and creating routines that feel good to you.

You find your daily rituals soothing and nurturing, and you don't want to miss them. Whether it's watching television, reading, taking naps, watching movies, or working on the computer, you become anxious and unbalanced if anything interferes with your routines.

You have a tendency to leave important tasks undone until the last minute, and you focus your time and energy on daily routines and other nonessential activities.

Collecting things is a fun hobby for you (whether they are collectibles or you are simply collecting information about a topic), and you may have difficulty letting go of these things. When it comes to prioritizing, you have a weakness for not being able to discern what's really important (to keep) and what's disposable (to throw out).

It's important to always have your needs met, and you will make sure that your home, car, office, purse, etc. are stocked with whatever supplies or resources you feel you might want. This may include your favourite treats because food is very important to you. You use food and eating to escape from things you find uncomfortable, to numb yourself, and to avoid or suppress your feelings.

In Relationships

When in love, you feel united with your beloved. In any other type of relationship, you want to merge with the other person—whether it's a friend, mentor, guru, a pet, nature, or a higher power. This unification feels heavenly to you; when you're not in a relationship, you may feel sad, lost, or yearning.

> You are always focused on your partner's needs and wants, and you will do whatever you can to make them happy.

It's important to avoid conflict with them because you believe you'll be happy if they are happy. Unfortunately, you become so attentive to your mate's every whim that you lose sight of what's going on with you, what you're feeling, what you want, etc.

And while you love catering to your partner's needs as you perceive them, you are not so eager to do as they ask! When your mate demands things of you, you become like a donkey and stubbornly digging your feet in. You may retreat emotionally and pull back from your partner or you may go along even though you secretly resent doing it.

When something goes wrong in your life, you have a habit of looking to blame someone else—and your beloved is typically the easiest and closest target. In order for you to grow, you need to learn to take responsibility for your role in the relationship, both good and bad.

Although you behave very dependently in your relationship, you may yearn to be more independent.

> You dream of someday knowing yourself fully and of understanding your desires, wishes, and vitality.

While you tend to deny your feelings, when you have a wide stretch of time to yourself, you can delve into your emotions and stay with them. Feelings are just something you're better able to experience when you're alone.

As you grow and evolve, you'll learn how to recognize your own needs, comprehend your own feelings, and speak up when you need to (without conflict). As you stand in your fullness, you will become a better and more fully present partner in your most intimate relationship.

Socially

As the social Nine, you join groups for many reasons. You like supporting a cause, but you also find that groups provide you with positive energy that feels good, offer you a venue to apply your skills and abilities, provide a sense of structure to your time, and help you learn where you might develop further as a person. Despite these benefits, sometimes you are ambivalent about whether you really want to belong!

In social settings, you may hang out on the edge of the party in order to keep from fully participating or committing yourself; this protective measure keeps you from being involved in any form of conflict. When people become rude or bossy, you are often left speechless, retreat, or become stubborn.

In a group environment, your default mode is to blend in or feel unimportant. Your attention is drawn externally to others (what's going on or any conflict or tension in the room) and away from your feelings and your inner world. Your constant external focus causes you to lose sight of your own views on life and to be unsure of your opinion or perspective on things.

Groups enjoy having you as a member because of your natural talents in mediating and building consensus. You sometimes take on the role of caretaker in your effort to be all things to all people. You sense so much about others' feelings and thoughts that you are quick to rush in and comfort or aid them. Ironically, you are the last one to know what you are thinking and feeling!

> Nine's worldview: Keep the peace and don't make trouble because my efforts won't make a difference.

Core Issues for Nines

Your basic fear is not being loved or not being able to give love. You worry that you'll be overlooked, ignored, or not valued. There is no other personality type who is so devoted to seeking internal and external peace, both for you and others.

You are so tuned in to other people's feelings, so caring and loving, but you worry that you will go without love. People enjoy your presence and your caring, nurturing manner. You are always welcomed into group settings, but you retreat, withdraw, and pull back from receiving all the love that is flowing towards you.

As you evolve and grow, you will discover that you can receive all the love you'll ever need through your spirituality and connection to the divine (as you define it) as well as by opening up and allowing the love from others to permeate and filter through to your heart.

When you feel connected, loved, and whole, you will be able to tune in to your own needs, wants, desires, and feelings more clearly, and you will feel more comfortable expressing yourself in the world.

> Once you are able to stand in your truth, you will find that you are equipped to succeed in a loving, intimate relationship.

You have been seeking comfort and harmony outside of yourself, but the secret is that it all can be found *inside* you. You are the one who creates harmony wherever you go; you are the one who comforts others and intuits their needs. You are the only one who can heal and love yourself! Go within to find all your answers.

Sample Questions

- How have I just gone along with others' opinions and ideas, even when I didn't agree?
- How much of my day did I spend on trivial matters that were not priorities?
- When did I become stubborn or feel resistant?
- Did my anger come up? If so, how and what did it look and feel like?
- How have I let my desire for comforts cause me to not take care of my basic needs (diet, exercise, etc.)?
- How did I respond when I sensed tension or conflict in the vicinity?

The Core of Healing

- Learn to place as much importance on *you* as you do on others.
- Get good at setting boundaries and limits—and at recognizing your priorities.
- Love yourself as much as you love others.
- Recognize that being uncomfortable and dealing with change are just parts of life.

Affirming Change

Affirmations, when used properly, are powerful tools for change. Affirmations are designed to speak directly to the subconscious mind and effect change on a level much deeper than your rational or conscious thoughts.

To use affirmations effectively, it's important to feel what you're saying and accept it as valid and real. Therefore, it's helpful to begin with an affirmation that allows you to release old beliefs and any thoughts that are no longer serving you. This is followed by a positive affirmation that brings in a new idea.

Once you feel comfortable saying the second affirmation, you can drop the first one and just use the second one:

- I release my need to ignore problems until they become overwhelming. I release my habit of not taking necessary action in my own life. I let go of the need to bury myself in mundane errands and to feel threatened by significant changes in my life.
- I am now awake to the world around me. I am a powerful healing force, always strong, confident, and independent. I am proud of myself and my abilities. All is well in my world.

Opportunities for Growth

As the peacemaking Nine, your desire to avoid conflict actually brings about the opposite effect; the fact that you avoid it causes others to have conflicts with you! It's important to comprehend that you will not have union with another until you have union with yourself (knowing, understanding, compassion, love of self).

Self-awareness and speaking your truth are not aggressive acts. They are positive ways of representing yourself in the world, allowing others to know and see you as you really are, being authentic and real, and valuing who you are and what you stand for.

Take a moment to reflect on your life. Has continually acquiescing to the wishes of others brought you the kind of connection and relationships you desire? Are you satisfied? If not, you will need to change what you're doing to get different results.

> Remember that it is not possible to love others if you are not allowing yourself to show up authentically and be fully present.

You need to be you—and be independent—in order to be available when others need you.

Demand more of yourself—and make yourself pay attention to what's happening around you without allowing yourself to tune out or stay on the fringe. Don't daydream, drift away, or retreat! Keep your attention focused and make yourself an active participant in life. Insist that you are mentally and emotionally engaged.

Tune in to your own emotions and acknowledge that you sometimes feel aggressive, anxious, or negative. You cannot effectively deal with these emotions by denying that they exist! You are human, and a complete range of feelings is to be expected.

Even though you pretended not to feel your negative emotions, you were still expressing them inadvertently—and people weren't fooled. Your repressed feelings create discord and disrupt the harmony you crave.

> Life will work better if you allow yourself to be open and honest about your feelings.

Before you can express them to others, you'll have to figure them out for yourself! Stop numbing yourself with television, computer, errands, and other trivial activities. Create some open space in your life and be receptive to delving into your depths.

Recognize the signs of passive-aggressive behaviour. If you slow down, refuse to take action, become stubborn, or dig your heels in, these are signs of anger. Understand that anger is really a good sign for you. When you feel angry, you know that you are aware of a previously hidden opinion, idea, or objection. It will only be a matter of time until you are clear and ready to share your perspective with others.

When it comes to making decisions, you are able to decide things more easily if you have choices to pick from. You know what you *don't* want more than what you *do* want. Instead of wondering what *others* want, stop and decide what *you* want.

If you get caught in an obsessive cycle of thought around making a decision, simply change your focus to another subject. Later, when your mind is calm, you can return and think about what you *don't* want as a way to discover your real desires.

Pay attention when you are using others as a reason for choosing a specific action. Stop and decide if you agree with them before choosing whether to go along with them or not.

Continue to rely on the structure of deadlines and the good feelings of positive feedback to help you achieve your goals and priorities.

> Notice when you're spinning your wheels on inconsequential things
> instead of emphasising your real priorities.

If you have been having relationship difficulties with a spouse, children, or friends, you will want to assess your role in the problem. Although this may be painful, it is a necessary part of growth. You have a tendency to blame everyone else, but in order to evolve, you will need to start taking your share of the responsibility for a relationship's success or failure. If you truly love the other person, you will walk through the challenging places in the short run in order to benefit the relationship and your well-being in the long run.

Lastly, it's critical for you to exercise regularly to stay in touch with your physical body and your emotions. Running errands is not exercise! When you create a connection with your body (body awareness), you have better concentration and the ability to focus your attention more easily. Physical exercise is a great way to vent any negative emotions you're having!

Stages of Evolution

For every personality type, there are opportunities to live from several different stages of growth, depending on whether you are reflective and interested in growing or are happy with the status quo. In addition, not everyone who is a Nine will have every trait or quality described here. Some will have traces of a characteristic, and others will see that same characteristic in abundance. A general overview of each stage is followed by a more detailed description.

Deteriorating

Unresponsive, fatalistic, unaware, oblivious, slothful, lazy, doubtful, fearful of catastrophe, suspicious, unable to tolerate conflict, passive, numb, neglectful, punitive, shut down, afraid of being unloved, disconnected, defiant, forgetful, commit crimes of omission, unable to face problems, highly repressed, undeveloped, ineffectual, dangerous to others, dissociated, can't function, depersonalized, severely disoriented, abandon self, shattered shell of a person, catatonic

> Your fear of being separate and alone underlies the way you interact with the world.

In order to feel included and accepted, you overlook or ignore your own needs and focus your attention on how you can accommodate others' needs and wishes. Ironically, this will not lead you to a union with another. It will cause you to lose yourself in the relationship, and the other person will never know who you really are. You will feel resentful when you wake up one day and realize what you gave up for them!

You try to avoid conflict and anxiety by removing yourself emotionally from any participation or engagement. If you can ignore the real issues, they might just go away. Even with this coping technique, after a while your anxieties, frustrations, and fears crescendo and become overwhelming.

The usually placid and stable Nine can become irritable, worried, and defensive as you begin to see everyone else as the causes of your discomfort. You begin complaining and blaming others for your distress.

> You may point the finger at authorities and blame them for having power over you.

If you experience this level of stress for a prolonged period of time, you can completely lose your calm manner and become overly nervous, testy, and reactive.

Even if you seek help from others at this point, you will turn on them and criticize them for telling you what to do or for dominating you! You really just want to block out anything that is affecting you. You may begin to dissociate until you can no longer function and become numb and withdrawn.

At your worst, you may pull back from society and your feelings so severely that you become totally disoriented, abandon yourself, and become a shell of your former self. You may even become catatonic.

Status Quo

Passive-aggressive, stubborn, inattentive, self-deprecating, ornery, obstinate, appeasing, resigned, wishful thinking, magical solutions, procrastinating, retreating, unresponsive, minimize problems, unreflective, complacent, hazy thinking, fantasizing, turn blind eye, unreliable, callous, indifferent, paralysed by decision-making, indolent, disengaged, self-forgetting

You feel unseen and unimportant; it is as though your views and opinions aren't heard or even worth saying aloud. You only attempt to show your appeal, values, and worthiness to your closest loved ones. Even then, you have no real sense of how you're coming across to them.

You avoid conflict at all costs. You idealize others and go along with their wishes in the hopes of pleasing them, avoiding disagreements, and making them happy with you.

When you are stressed, you may work harder and become even more productive; unfortunately, your production is usually just a lot of busywork that makes you feel like you're accomplishing something, but it doesn't contribute significantly to the actual outcome.

> Staying perpetually busy is a habit that keeps you from feeling your emotions.

Busying yourself, becoming more productive and achieving is how you build up your self-confidence and self-esteem. Being busy allows you to delude yourself into thinking that you don't have any problems and that you are truly peaceful. If the negative feelings push too much on you, you may retreat into delusions and fantasies as a way to escape and tune out reality.

Co-workers may become frustrated by your lack of productivity—despite your stressed-out, overworked, frazzled demeanour! They may feel that you are not pulling your weight or that you are too quick to blame them for things that are your responsibility.

You can become obstinate and ineffectual from all the stress. Your coping technique is to disengage and pay less attention to life. In order to feel safe and unaffected, you pull back and become complacent and unresponsive. Your thinking may become hazy and muddled.

The Alarm

When you become aware of your continual need to accommodate others at your expense, you can wake up and realize that you are just as valuable as anyone else is. You will see that your thoughts and opinions matter—and that you are strong, worthy, and significant. When you fully internalize this and live from your inner power, the peace-loving Nine is in the unique position to truly be able to bring peace and harmony to the world.

Evolving

Unifying, appreciative, genuine, protective, peaceful, content, in the flow of life, welcoming, accommodating, harmonious, sharing, feel valued, loving, loved, healthy self-esteem, enjoy life, agreeable, natural, comfortable, calm, unassuming, approachable, considerate, gentle, empathizing, intuitive, steady, good mediator, peacemaker

You are emotionally sound and stable, know how to trust others and yourself, and are at ease with life and comfortable with your own feelings.

> You live simply and purely with an unpretentious approach to life.

You are kind and patient with people, supportive of their wishes, and clear about your own needs and boundaries. You understand people's emotions on a deep, empathic, intuitive level and are receptive and open. People love to be around you!

Your optimistic outlook, healing influence, and ability to bring harmony to diverse situations enables you to bring people closer together, find a middle ground, and facilitate compromises that are in everyone's best interests.

You are an excellent peacemaker, communicator, and synthesizer and distiller of wants and needs. You are accepting of all points of view, and people respect you and your natural gifts.

On Your Spiritual Path

Easy-going, humble, not self-conscious, accepting, unpretentious, self-effacing, gracious, patient, compromising, at ease, reassuring, embracing, receptive, appreciative, engaged, clear about values, in touch with own emotions, connected, decisive, self-aware, present, optimistic, creative, stable, self-possessed, autonomous, alive, serene, innocent, genuine

Your goal is to bring harmony to the world and to help people find peaceful solutions to conflicts. You realize your worth, value, and potential to help others, and you are now comfortable standing in your truth and sharing your gifts with people.

> You know that your very presence on the earth makes you valuable and loved.

On a deep level, you understand that you are making an important contribution to humanity. You've come to the conclusion that the peace of mind you so desperately sought comes from gifting the world with your abilities and skills and from sharing yourself freely.

You have come full circle and are able to recognize and take pleasure in your own value, worth, and goodness. You are self-possessed and confident. Life fulfils you, and you know what it means to love yourself and to love and be loved by others.

You've learned that you are able to form profound intimate connections with others by becoming comfortable with yourself and clearly defining your needs. You are fully alive, vibrant, engaged, and fulfilled. You have finally become a true mediator for the world.

Type Nine: The Mediator

As the supportive, accepting Nine, you are able to empathize with others more than most other personality types can. As a result, people really enjoy your company. You make them feel special, heard, valued, and loved.

However, this peace-loving nature of yours also has a downside—you find conflict intensely distressing and will avoid it at all costs. You will go along to get along instead of making your views and ideas known. In the end, no one will really know who you are—and neither will you!

Your overwhelming desire to love and be loved will be jeopardized because your partner can't truly know you when they can't truly love you. You will wake up one day and feel resentful that your mate doesn't really see you—and you'll place the blame at his or her feet.

> You'll end up feeling alone and unseen when all you had to do was learn to love yourself and value your own contributions!

Once you grow and evolve to the point of being in touch with your emotions, opinions, wishes, and needs, you will learn to feel comfortable expressing yourself, taking a stand, and dealing with disagreements along the way.

> Your growth depends on you reclaiming yourself, awakening from your lethargic fog, and engaging fully in life.

You are here to make significant contributions to humanity through your amazing talents for peacemaking, reaching compromises in difficult situations, helping people feel heard and understood, and creating workable solutions.

You can step fully onto your path once you have defined your sense of self and learned to stand in your truth, proud (in a humble, self-effacing way) of your gifts and talents, and ready to share them with others as the true mediator you are here to be.

About the Author

With Joanne Antoun's guidance, you are guaranteed to step into your power and live the life you dream.

Joanne is a lecturer in the field of personal growth and consciousness, and she is the creator and trainer of the two-hour life-transforming Combined Therapy Cocktail (CTC).

She is also a psychotherapist, Reiki master teacher, NLP master practitioner and trainer, hypnotherapy trainer, EFT trainer, life coach, motivational and inspirational speaker, teacher of accelerated learning techniques, and author.

Joanne brings highly intuitive abilities and an in-depth spiritual perspective into everything she does. She captivates her audiences with her quick wit and easy-going style. Her kind-hearted approach to issues and limiting beliefs makes it easy to evaluate and release them, allowing people to discover and live their true potential.

Joanne is available for personal sessions of CTC, workshops, seminars, and corporate events.

You have the book, and you'll love the matching phone app. Check out the *Life Guide* app now. Visit www.joanneantoun.com.